T0049690

The United States
of Cryptids

– THE –
UNITED STATES *of*
CRYPTIDS

A TOUR OF AMERICAN
MYTHS AND MONSTERS

J. W. Ocker

QUIRK BOOKS
PHILADELPHIA

Library of Congress Cataloging-in-Publication Data
Names: Ocker, J. W., author.
Title: The United States of cryptids : a tour of American myths and monsters / J.W. Ocker.
Description: Philadelphia : Quirk Books, [2022] | Includes bibliographical references and index. | Summary: "A guide to cryptids of the United States and the local communities that celebrate them" —Provided by publisher.
Identifiers: LCCN 2022012464 (print) | LCCN 2022012465 (ebook) | ISBN 9781683693222 (hardcover) | ISBN 9781683693239 (ebook)
Subjects: LCSH: Cryptozoology. | Monsters—United States. | Animals—United States—Folklore.
Classification: LCC QL89 .O25 2022 (print) | LCC QL89 (ebook) | DDC 001.944—dc23/eng/20220528
LC record available at https://lccn.loc.gov/2022012464
LC ebook record available at https://lccn.loc.gov/2022012465

ISBN: 978-1-68369-322-2

Printed in China

Typeset in Vertrina, Battlefin, Novel, and Novel Sans

Designed by Elissa Flanigan
Illustrations by Derek Quinlan
Production management by John J. McGurk

Quirk Books
215 Church Street
Philadelphia, PA 19106
quirkbooks.com

10 9 8 7 6 5 4 3

To Alex Slater

For helping me unleash so many of my own monsters

Contents

III. The Midwest

Your Backyard Is Full of Monsters

I n March 1960, I set out on my journey to investigate the hidden monsters of the world. At the time, I knew realistically that the classic celebrity cryptids—the Loch Ness Monster, the Himalayan abominable snowpeople (yeti), and the great sea serpents—were out of reach for me. I was born into a Navy family in Norfolk, Virginia, and I grew up among the soybean fields of Decatur, Illinois. From there, even the bigfoot territory of the Pacific Northwest seemed a long way off.

But I did what I could, starting in my own midwestern backyard—which, it turns out, hid plenty of monsters to keep me busy. I even chose to go to Southern Illinois University in Carbondale because of the rich folklore and history there about red swamp apes and backwoods black panther sightings.

I got rides from family or hitchhiked to midwestern cryptid encounter sites. Eventually, I did travel across the country and the world to indulge my fascination with the overlooked and the alleged. Along the way, as I witnessed the evidence of mysterious creatures on the landscape, I also witnessed the field of cryptozoology grow and evolve and become mainstream enough that you could find these creatures in souvenir shops and at festivals, too. But, for me, it all started as a local mission.

And I believe that's the same spirit that imbues this book you hold in your hands. J. W. Ocker, with his enjoyable and distinctive sensibility, wonderfully details and documents how vast the United States is when it comes to monsters. How full of encounters and stories, yes, but also, uniquely, how packed the land is with cryptid statues, monster museums, and annual events dedicated to them. That means those who are intrigued by the topic have much more exposure and access to the wonders of cryptozoology than that curious young man in the mid-century Midwest.

Today, there are lots of ways to pursue your own adventures into cryptozoological science, whether it's a trek into the dense forest or a trip to a town square. And it's a stranger and better world for it.

Enjoy the quest,
Loren Coleman
International Cryptozoology
 Museum
Portland and Bangor, Maine
February 14, 2022

Guaranteed to See a Cryptid or Your Money Back

B igfoot exists: definitely, demonstrably, unequivocally. So do lake dinosaurs, monster cats, jet-sized birds, lizard-people, fish-people, wolf-people, moth-people, frog-people, and goat-people. All cryptids exist. Let me prove it to you. Wait, no—let me show them to you. But first: What the heck's a cryptid?

A cryptid is a creature or species whose existence is scientifically unproven. Maybe it's been witnessed or rumored to exist, maybe it's even been caught on video, but there is no definitive physical evidence to examine: no body to dissect, no remains to analyze. Scientists place those creatures in the category of fantasy instead of zoology. Cryptozoologists, though, who study and pursue cryptids, place them in the entirely separate category of cryptozoology. While the fantastical Mothman and the Jersey Devil may be the first cryptids you think of, a cryptid can be as comparatively mundane as a New England panther or an American lion; animals that once existed but are now believed by the scientific establishment to be extinct. Sometimes these animals are even discovered: the coelacanth, a fish thought to have gone extinct in the age of the dinosaurs, was discovered alive in 1938. A cryptid can even be an ordinary animal that is supposedly thriving where it couldn't be, like a population of alligators in the Manhattan sewers, or freshwater octopuses.

At least, that's the traditional definition of a cryptid. Since cryptozoology was established in its modern form in the fifties, the definition has widened to encompass even more fantastical creatures as more people grow interested in the topic. This includes extraterrestrial entities, creatures from folklore such as mermaids and gnomes, sentient non-humans like the Menehune of Hawaii, and even (possibly) robots. This expanding definition of cryptid isn't just because cryptozoology fans are a welcoming lot. It's because *cryptid* has become synonymous with *monster*, of any kind. Cryptid fans love monsters, and pop culture cryptozoology is basically Pokémon: we want to collect all the monster stories, and we want the widest variety of them in our collection as possible.

It's a messy word, cryptid. But that's what makes it fun. Most of us who heart cryptids are fine with that imprecision and aren't overly invested in the -ology part of cryptozoology. We don't camp out for weeks in dense forests knocking on trees and scrounging for bigfoot scat. We don't charter boats and rent side-scan sonar systems to scrutinize lake bottoms for water monsters. Unlike cryptozoologists, we aren't trying to scientifically prove the existence of cryptids—we just love the idea of them; we love the stories. And, whatever you think about cryptids, the stories are true. You may disbelieve that a lizard man attacked a car in a South Carolina swamp in the summer of 1988, but the Lizard Man mania is irrefutably documented. In other words, the story is true, regardless of whether the Lizard Man itself is real.

But I promised to show you cryptids, not just tell you about them. We're going to focus on these fantastic beasts where we can actually find them: in the towns that claim and celebrate them, that hallow the ground of the sighting, that tie their local cryptid to their identity and geography, and that capitalize on them economically. And for whatever reason, America does cryptotourism best and biggest (apologies to Loch Ness). According to a 2018 estimate by Loren Coleman, founder of the International Cryptozoology Museum in Portland, Maine, cryptotourism generates as much as $140 million annually in the United States. And those tourists aren't merely following tour guides into the wilderness to prove that mosquitoes exist while looking for hairy hominids. They're partying at a festival dedicated to an alien pterodactyl that terrorized the town for five days a hundred years ago. They're pulling up to the counter at a lake-monster-themed eatery in a county whose biggest export is a whopper of a story. They're buying T-shirts and plushies at a monster museum in the middle of nowhere dedicated to a giant insect. They're going to Cryptid Towns.

But sanctifying your snallygasters isn't just tourist-trapping or trappings for tourists. Embracing a local monster can bring a community together around a shared identity. Outside of sports teams, that can be difficult to come by these days. But if you're the town that found a giant turtle living in your local pond in the 1970s or were attacked by a vampire cat in the 1950s? That's yours alone to own, and you can name a park after it, theme a business around it, build a museum or a statue honoring it, and propose legislation to protect it and its habitat. Wherever cryptids are celebrated, the story is so much more important than the science.

I've seen many of these places personally. If you tell me there's a hodag statue in Wisconsin, I want to see it with my own eyes, same as if you told me there was an actual hodag in Wisconsin. In South Dakota, I took selfies with the world's largest chainsaw bigfoot sculpture. In Vermont, I hiked an icy mountaintop to find Wampahoofus Trail. In Ohio, I climbed an ancient mound shaped like an underwater panther. I have been to many cryptid museums and gift shops, and I have a shelf full of souvenirs to prove it. I sometimes joke that when I say I'm hunting cryptids, what I mean is that I'm driving to a town to drink a craft beer named after one. But I did also venture into their territories. After dark, I entered the old cement bunkers in the West Virginia forest that are the lair of the Mothman. I boated from New York to Vermont across Lake Champlain looking for sinuous humps in the water. I walked through an Arizona canyon that skinwalkers are known to haunt—but only after I drove to town to see if they had any craft beers named after them.

Sadly, not every town with a cryptid story commemorates it. But I haven't left those cryptids out of this book. It's not their fault. I tell the stories of these unsung cryptids and pitch the reasons why they deserve to be turned into local attractions. And if one of these towns erects so much as an informational sign in honor of their monster because of this book, then I count this project a success, regardless of the metrics of my publisher.

But cryptids exist in yet another way beyond stories and monuments. Many who love cryptids love them more as symbols of the natural world than as secrets of it. Cryptids are hopeful concepts: hope that the world is still a diverse place full of discovery. Hope that humankind hasn't zoned every square inch of the planet for McDonald's franchises. Hope that we haven't grown bored with our mother planet, that she still harbors wonders for us. Cryptids exist: as stories, as monuments, as symbols. Maybe even as more than that. But those three ways already make them as much a part of this planet as any officially acknowledged creature in a zoology textbook. Now, let's go party with some monsters. Because we're going to find them—guaranteed.

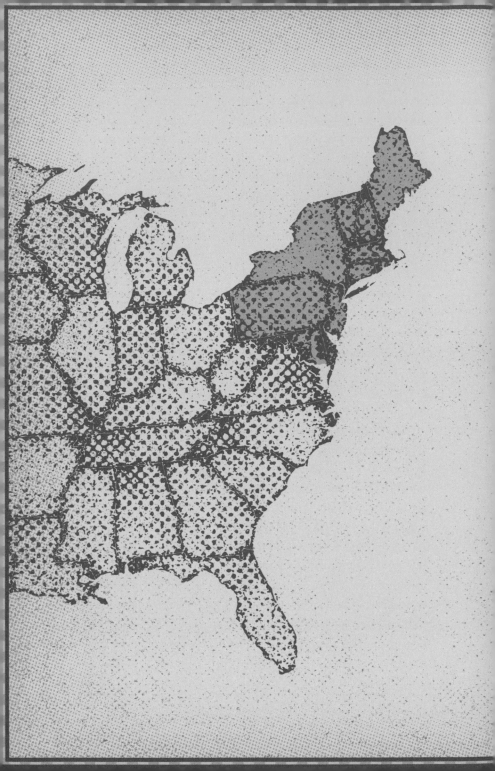

PART I.

THE NORTHEAST

The northeast region of the United States is the oldest part of the country. Much of it was colonized by black-clad religious folks who saw Satan-sent monsters behind every tree in this scary, dark, cold New World. These days the Northeast is much different from what those original settlers found, but it has maintained its monsters. Like, a lot of them, especially considering that the Northeast is also the smallest region in the country. Among the cryptids found here are the best-documented aquatic cryptids on the continent, a devil of a state mascot, and, somehow, somehow, somehow, the most important site in the entire United States of Cryptids.

– Champ –

AMERICA'S LOCH NESS MONSTER

TYPE:	EARLIEST SIGHTING:
Aquatic	1819
LOCATION:	**SIZE:**
Burlington, Vermont; Port Henry, New York	15–50 feet long

Imagine a tug of war between the residents of two differ-ent towns in two different states on opposite shores of a massive lake. Instead of a rope, they're tugging a giant, scaly sea serpent back and forth. That's what's happening right now on Lake Champlain as both Port Henry, New York, and Burlington, Vermont, try to champion Champ the Lake Monster as their own.

Not all lakes deserve their own monsters, but Lake Champlain certainly does. It covers 435 square miles, drops to a depth of 400 feet, and contains almost 7 trillion gallons of monster-loving water. It has 587 miles of shoreline, more than seventy islands, and borders two states and Canada. It's one of the largest lakes in the country. If you can't hide a lake monster here, you can't a hide a lake monster anywhere. But its lake monster is not exactly hidden.

Sightings began in the early nineteenth century and spanned the length of the lake. A scow captain named Crum caught sight of the monster in Bulwagga Bay, on the New York side. In the *Plattsburgh Republican*, he described it as "about 187 feet long, its head flat with three teeth, two in the under and one in the upper jaw . . . the color black, with a star in the forehead and a belt of red around the neck . . . the eyes large and the color of peeled onion." Railroad workers on the shores of Dresden, New York, saw a massive, fish-tailed serpent swimming toward them. University students in Burlington, Vermont, witnessed the creature slicing through the water, a good fifteen feet of its head and neck visible. Most of the accounts are similar, featuring boaters or picnickers or vacationers who see a large-headed serpentine creature minding its own business on the water. Eventually, the creature became so famous that P. T. Barnum, showman and founder of the famous Barnum & Bailey Circus, wrote the *Whitehall Times* of New York and offered a $50,000 reward for "the hide of the great Champlain serpent."

Over the centuries, descriptions of the beast have evolved from a here be monsters–style humped sea serpent to a slightly more scientific-seeming oceanic dinosaur (or technically, an extinct marine reptile) with a long neck, bulbous body, and flippers—a plesiosaur. And while a dinosaur in a lake is just as strange as a sea serpent in a lake, cryptozoologists remind us that Lake Champlain and surrounding parts of Vermont, New York, and Canada were once submerged under the Champlain Sea, which extended to the Atlantic Ocean during the last ice age. Multiple ancient whale skeletons from this period have been found in Vermont, including the Charlotte whale, a beluga skeleton discovered in 1849 that today is the state marine fossil.

Over the past two centuries, sightings have waxed and waned like the humps on Champ's own back, totaling a few hundred according to some tallies. And then, in the late twentieth century, the Champ case was bestowed that holy grail of cryptozoology: a blurry photograph.

On July 5, 1977, a vacationing tourist named Sandra Mansi was picnicking on the shores of the Vermont side of Champlain, near St. Albans, with her family. She saw a large brown head on a long neck breach the water. She grabbed her Kodak Instamatic and shot a photo that became almost as legendary as the "surgeon's photo," the best-known photograph of the Loch Ness Monster (which was acknowledged as a hoax decades later). Mansi's Kodak moment—which had the benefit of being in full color—has never had that kind of reckoning and was featured everywhere from *Time* magazine to the *New York Times*. Champ was dubbed "America's Loch Ness Monster."

With sightings, documentation, and publicity of Champ spanning centuries, it's no wonder that more than one town on the lake has a Barnum level of lust for the creature. In Burlington, Vermont, they've erected a gravestone-like monument to the lake monster. It bears a cartoony image of Champ and its pseudoscientific name: *Belua aquatica champlainiensis*. The city also named its minor league baseball team after the creature: the Vermont Lake Monsters, since a sports team named "the Champs" would get made fun of every time they lost. ECHO, a science and nature museum right on the shore, showcases an exhibit on the monster (and plenty of Champ toys in the gift shop). The exhibit sits adjacent to a tank of live sturgeons, large fishes with bumps on their backs called scutes, which are one of the creatures skeptics believe people mistake for Champ.

In Port Henry, New York, they put Champ on the town welcome sign and declared their waters a safe haven for it. The sign for the Chamber of Commerce features an illustration of the town on the back of a plesiosaur. They celebrate a Champ Day every year that features a parade in honor of the beast. They erected a board on the edge of town that lists every sighting through August 1989. The very first sighting is attributed to explorer Samuel de Champlain. In 1609, he became the first European to see the lake and is the man for whom both Lake Champlain and, indirectly, its monster are named. Unfortunately, the Champ sighting story is an apocryphal one, deriving from a 1970 issue of *Vermont Life* magazine that erroneously references the explorer's journal.

If you meander around either Burlington or Port Henry, you'll have plenty of Champ sightings. Scattered throughout are statues of Champ and artwork dedicated to it and various businesses wrapped in its serpentine coils. But even these two towns need to be wary of competition. Lake Champlain is big—a lot of towns touch its shoreline. An hour north of Port Henry, in Plattsburgh, New York, a historical sign commemorating "Champy," funded by the state's Legends and Lore program, is planted against the backdrop of the lake.

I'm tempted to say that whoever celebrates Champ the most should win that tug of war across the lake, but both Burlington and Port Henry are advocating admirably for Champ's legacy. I guess if you can share an amazing lake, you can share an amazing lake monster.

–Wampahoofus–

THE MISALIGNED MOUNTAINEERS

TYPE:	EARLIEST SIGHTING:
Mammalian	19th century
LOCATION:	**NOTABLE FEATURE:**
Underhill, Vermont	Legs shorter on one side

It's a lot easier to find the trail of a cryptid when that trail is marked and labeled. For example: Wampahoofus Trail on Vermont's Mount Mansfield.

The wampahoofus is a large mammal of vague description, possibly like a deer or a goat or even a boar. The ambiguity is due to the fact that documented encounters are rare or nonexistent. Its defining characteristic, though, is its legs. They are shorter on one side than on the other. On flat land, those uneven legs make the beast like a bicycle without a kickstand—unable to hold itself upright. However, the asymmetry is uniquely adapted to the steep hills and mountains that are its natural terrain. Other names for the creature include side-hill gouger and gyascutus, and in Henry Tyron's 1939 compendium of lumberjack lore, *Fearsome Critters*, he also offers godaphro, side-hill wowser, prock, and side-hill badger—all subpar appellations, in my opinion, to the delightful-sounding wampahoofus.

Lots of states claim similar animals, which explains some of the name variations, but the creature seems to have originated in Vermont. Tyron quotes a man by the name of Bill Ericsson from North Haven, Maine, to explain how these lopsided creatures might have migrated across flat land to mountains in other states. According to Ericsson, the beasts compensated for their shortened sides by leaning those short sides against each other, with their longer legs on the outside, stabilizing each other "like a pair of drunks going home from town." Nature finds a way.

But the life of the wampahoofus isn't all idyllic gambols around mountainsides. Because of their unique leg structures, a wampahoofus can move in only one direction around a mountain. Attempting to turn around with those lopsided legs inevitably causes them to topple down the mountainside to their deaths. Other accounts claim that males and females have opposing short sides (left for females, right for males). That means males can only travel clockwise around a mountain and females counterclockwise, meeting at opportune times to mate. Still others believe that which sides are short and which are long is a random trait and not a marker of sex. That means any two wampahoofuses can meet, and when they do (and if they are not ready to start a family), they must fight to the death since neither can turn around. It's no wonder these animals are so rare as to be cryptozoological. As strange as the idea of bilaterally asymmetrical legs is, though, it is not unprecedented as a scientific theory. Some seventeenth-century naturalists hypothesized that the decidedly un-cryptozoological badger had uneven legs, explaining how it could clamber up and down hills so rapidly.

Back at Wampahoofus Central, Mount Mansfield is the tallest point in Vermont (3,943 feet above sea level), and its peaks vaguely form the shape of a face, with each peak bearing the name of a facial feature—forehead, chin, and nose. Long Trail runs the length of the visage, while Wampahoofus Trail cuts across it (just follow the blue blazes). It's a bit of a hike to get to the trail, and it's not an easy one. It involves scrambling across vertiginous rocks slippery from snow and winter run-off, few flat surfaces, and lots of panicked wandering and sweaty wondering if this stupid beast is even worth this trek to include in your book. Obviously, it'll help if one of your legs is shorter than the other.

No promises that you'll see a wampahoofus on Wampahoofus Trail, though. Rumor has it that inbreeding between opposite-legged wampahoofuses created offspring with legs either too short to be of use, or with short and long legs mixed at random on both sides, creating snaggle-legged wampahoofuses and resulting in the extinction of the species. I guess they just couldn't find a leg to stand on.

– Whitehall Bigfoot –

THE COPS VS. SASQUATCH

TYPE:	EARLIEST SIGHTING:
Humanoid	1976
LOCATION:	**SIZE:**
Whitehall, New York	7–8 feet tall

It's extremely possible, in the town of Whitehall, New York, to see more bigfoot than people on any given day: at the liquor store, at the golf course, at the local park. The reason why dates back half a century. Whitehall is eighty miles north of Albany, barely across the border from Vermont and in the foothills of the Adirondacks. The Champlain Canal that wends through the town is connected to the plesiosaur-infested waters of Lake Champlain (see page 18), and the surrounding woods are the perfect place for a monster to hide.

On the night of August 24, 1976, teenagers Paul Gosselin and Martin Paddock were driving around the lonely roads through the farmlands outside of town on their way to do some fishing. On Abair Road, they encountered a monster. They heard it first—a sound like the squeal of a pig or the scream of a woman in distress. They loaded their shotguns and turned the truck around to see. And what they saw was humanlike, muscular, seven or eight feet tall, with dark fur and red eyes. You know the guy: Bigfoot. It charged them, so they peeled out of there.

Leaving a black trail of burned rubber behind them, they

encountered Paul's twenty-four-year-old brother Brian Gosselin—an officer with the local police department—manning a speed trap. Brian dutifully reported the monster sighting, first calling up his father, a police sergeant in Whitehall, and then the state police and sheriff's department. He couldn't check out the area himself because he was on duty and had to stay in the village. Meanwhile, Paul and Martin picked up their friend Bart Kinny, drove back to Abair Road, and encountered the creature again. Eventually, an old-fashioned search party of about a dozen people was formed on Abair Road. Some of the party, including police officers, saw the creature across the meadow, but it was long gone before they could catch up to it.

The next day, Brian Gosselin revisited the scene with a state trooper. He had a much closer encounter, spotlighting the creature with his flashlight from thirty feet away. It screamed, threw its hands in front of its face, and then walked off into the woods. Later, in writing about the encounter in his book *Abair Road: The True Story*, Gosselin attempted to explain his reaction: "I can't really describe what I was feeling, shock and yes, fear. I was face-to-face with something that shouldn't exist but it was right there in front of me."

Over the next week, several people in the area around Abair Road reported seeing a large, dark creature loping through the forests and fields. Some ran from it, others shot at it. A large print was found not too far from the road in a mossy log. UFOs were also spotted in the skies. It was a real moment for the town. But after that week, most people kept quiet about the unsettling events. The police involvement made the incident noteworthy, but it also became embarrassing for the town and the police force. Eventually, the town's attitude toward its local legend turned from shame to fame due to wider acceptance of bigfoot across the country—both as a cryptozoological phenomenon and a pop culture one—as well as the economic need for tourists. Bigfoot sightings in the area have been reported sporadically in the years since, even as recently as August 2018, when a driver saw a large, black, hairy form climbing over a guardrail at night on Route 4.

Today, Abair Road is still surrounded by farmland and forest, but to see bigfoot you gotta head downtown. Four large bigfoot statues are scattered throughout Whitehall, and not the pre-fab ones you can buy on any internet novelty site: we're talking big, custom creatures, no two alike. A nine-foot-tall chainsaw sculpture of a bigfoot looms in Riverside Park. A hulking metal gorilla of a bigfoot with a bigfoot baby on its back dominates the parking lot outside of the Vermont Marble Granite, Slate & Soapstone Co., a masonry store that doubles as a bigfoot gift shop. The third statue serves as a mascot for Bigfoot Liquors. The fourth is at the first hole of the Skene Valley Country Club golf course, a metal beast complete with a flag in one hand and a golf club in the other. This one marks the site of a bigfoot sighting by golf course owner Cliff Sparks, about a year before the incident at Abair Road. The bigfoot he saw had red laser beams shooting from its eyes.

But the town has done more than erect metal and wooden monsters. They've passed legislation to protect bigfoot, officially named it the town animal, and named 5K runs and golf tournaments after it. They've even jumpstarted a Sasquatch Calling Festival, where everybody tries out their best bigfoot call. Brian Gosselin, who would know, has judged the contest in the past.

Before the folks in Whitehall started calling out to bigfoot instead of running from them, the town's biggest claim to fame was as the birthplace of the US Navy, a dubitable claim shared by half a dozen places in the country. Being a Cryptid Town is much more fun, and Whitehall proves that it's never too late to embrace your monster. And if you have police witnesses of it, even better.

– Silver Lake Serpent –

FAKING A HOAX

TYPE:	EARLIEST SIGHTING:
Aquatic	1855
LOCATION:	**SIZE:**
Perry, New York	60 feet long

Nobody in Perry, New York, believes there is a monster in Silver Lake. At least, they haven't since 1857, when it became widely understood that the sightings two years earlier were an admitted, proven hoax. But Perry doesn't care: it still makes a big deal out of the fake creature more than a century and a half later.

Perry is forty-five miles south of Rochester. Its defining feature is the long, thin Silver Lake on its western border. It's not a big lake. It averages seventeen feet in depth and only covers an area of about 836 acres. But it was lake enough for a monster—or at least a monster story.

On the night of July 13, 1855, five men and two boys rowed out to fish Silver Lake, but they ended up being the ones that got away. What they at first took to be a log floating in the water suddenly swam toward the boat, rearing up when it got close to reveal itself as a giant finned serpent as thick as a barrel. This sighting was no mere humps in the distance or misidentified sturgeon. This monster was right up in their faces while they quaked in their boat, and then almost capsized the boat with its splashing. They oared to shore in horror, telling their tale as soon as they hit land like a group of Jonahs fresh from the belly of the whale. Some even signed sworn affidavits of their testimony.

A few days later, the monster appeared again, this time before a family enjoying a boat ride on the lake. And then it appeared again. And again. But the real activity was on dry land, as tourists and monster hunters flocked to the lake, filling local hotels, building watchtowers, and carrying around harpoons like small-town Ahabs. Various newspapers reported that a reward had been offered for the serpent's capture (one dollar per foot of hide, with a minimum of sixty feet). The *Buffalo Daily Republic* even suggested that the local Perry newspaper needed to either establish a daily edition or string a telegraph line so that its insatiable readers could get more frequent reports of the monstrous goings-on.

Then, in 1857, the Walker Hotel, one of the local establishments that had been doing a brisk business serving the lake monster crowds, caught fire. What the firefighters found among the ashes (or lodged in the attic, depending on the account) was the makings of a monster: singed canvas and wire shaped like a large sea serpent. The proprietor of the hotel, Artemis Walker, admitted that he and some associates had created the serpent back in 1855 to drum up business. Those smoky remnants were once a sixty-foot-long creature, green with yellow spots, and bright red eyes and mouth. It was made of waterproof canvas wrapped around coils of wire that was sunk with weights to the bottom of the relatively shallow lake. The canvas was connected to a hose leading to a massive blacksmith bellows hidden in a shanty on shore. The bellows pushed air through the hose, inflating the beast so that it would rise and terrorize lakegoers. A set of ropes leading to shore was used to maneuver the monster. When the bellows ceased, the deflated canvas sunk back into the dark water, dragged down to the bottom by the weights.

Despite the proof and the admission of the hoax, Perry still celebrates that pile of burnt canvas and wire today. You can't turn your head downtown without seeing the Silver Lake Serpent—it's featured on welcome signs, the town seal, the bike racks, and various local businesses. Perry also proudly displays three different statues: a cartoony beast on a playground splash pad that shoots water out of its mouth, a more foreboding statue that loops into and out of the ground at the edge of a golf course, and a metal art installation downtown. The Pioneer Cabin and Museum in Perry even has in its collection artifacts from that heady mid-nineteenth century event, including the bellows that supposedly gave the cryptid life and one of the harpoons meant to take it away.

In the 1960s, Perry started throwing a killer festival in the serpent's honor, with a Sea Serpent Queen and a parade that featured large reproductions of the creature as floats or pageant puppets. The monster made for the 1962 parade burned to ash when the building it was housed in burned down, mimicking the 1857 fire. The monster built for the 1978 parade also ended up catching fire and burning, as did the monster from the 1980 parade. The town stopped celebrating the festival after a few decades, although it was rekindled in 2020, complete with the traditional reproduction of the sea serpent. Which they burned afterward—on purpose this time.

An interesting coda to this story comes from professional skeptic Joe Nickell. Nickell has spent his life debunking the paranormal, throwing his wet blanket atop sheet ghosts and cryptids wherever he finds them. In this case, in a fascinating reversal, he attempted to debunk not the monster, but the hoax. That's right: Joe Nickell, professional skeptic, doesn't believe that the Silver Lake Serpent was a hoax. Or at least not the hoax most consider it to be. In the March/April 1999 issue of *Skeptical Inquirer*, Nickell proposed that the Walker Hotel fire and subsequent reveal of the hoax never happened. He tracks the story to its first mention, an account in 1915, nearly sixty years after the event, by a local historian named Frank D. Roberts. Three things point to the story of the fake serpent being a hoax: the gap in time between the supposed fire and the first report of it, the difference between the descriptions of the canvas serpent and the serpent seen on the lake, and the implausibly complex mechanisms for operating the fake serpent. Does this mean the Silver Lake Sea Serpent was real after all? Perhaps. Or perhaps it was a hoax—just not one involving a hotel fire and an inflatable serpent.

This puts Perry, New York, in an extremely strange position: it's a town that celebrates either a lake monster that never existed, or a hoax that never happened. Which is a super-cool predicament—but hard to edit down into a town motto.

–Jersey Devil –

THE PINEY POLTERGEIST

TYPE:	EARLIEST SIGHTING:
Aerial	1735
LOCATION:	**NOTABLE FEATURES:**
Pine Barrens, New Jersey	Bipedal; horse-faced; bat wings

Anthony Bourdain sat here, where I was sitting, at the counter of this tiny diner in New Jersey. And you know what he talked about? Not just the food, but the Jersey Devil. Few cryptids have risen to such stardom in their home state as the Jersey Devil. It's synonymous with the place, almost a word association game answer.

The story of the Jersey Devil is a strange one: part colonial folklore, part classic cryptid sighting, and part supernatural boogeyman. It begins on a stormy night in 1735, in what would become the town of Leeds Point on the coast of southern New Jersey (another name for the creature is the Leeds Devil). Mother Leeds was pregnant with her thirteenth child, a thirteenth child she wasn't enthusiastic about. So she cursed it—and then she delivered a monster. It was horse-faced, long-necked, and horned, with bat wings, a forked tail, and two legs ending in hooves. And it was ferocious. It attacked everybody in the room, and then flapped up the chimney like a reverse Santa Claus into the storm to haunt the Pine Barrens.

The Pine Barrens is a protected area of coastal pines that covers one million acres and is rich with spooky history. Because of its resources, it was the site of major industries like shipbuilding, iron ore processing, and glassmaking. Because of its isolation, it was crammed with moonshine operations during Prohibition. The mafia even used it as a place to get rid of bodies. Today, it's a green, ghost-town-pocked oasis in an extremely developed part of the Eastern Seaboard: in other words, the perfect spot to hide a monster.

At this stage, the Jersey Devil is not yet a cryptid in the traditional sense, just a bit of supernatural folklore. However, some hypothesize that it didn't even originate as folklore, but rather as gossip or mockery about the real-life Leeds family of Leeds Point. The origin of the term "Leeds Devil" may have been a taunt against the Leeds for siding with England in the years leading up to the Revolutionary War. Regardless of the source of the name, it wasn't until the early twentieth century that the Jersey Devil emerged from hazy rumors to enter people's towns and homes.

For a week in January 1909, sightings of a strange flying beast that left cloven tracks in the snow occurred all over southern New Jersey and across the border in Pennsylvania. In Trenton, New Jersey, city councilman E. P. Weeden was awakened in the night by something beating at his door and the sound of wings in the air. He looked out an upper-story window and saw a line of bipedal hoofprints in the snow on his roof. Other people in Trenton heard strange screeches in the night, saw more hoofprints in the snow, or even witnessed the thing itself flapping in the night sky.

Meanwhile, just across the Delaware River in Bristol, Pennsylvania, police officer James Sackville got close enough to

shoot at it. Postmaster E. W. Minister described the monster as crane-like, with long wings and the horned head of a ram. He even claimed that it glowed with an unnatural light. Liquor store owner John McOwen saw something eagle-like hopping on the ground outside his window and described its cry as a phonograph record scratch combined with a factory whistle.

It didn't take long for everybody to connect the sightings to the old folktale and start screaming Devil. Schools and businesses across the region shut down. Hunting parties were formed. Fearful people armed themselves. And one person took advantage: his name was Norman Jefferies, and he was the publicist for a dime museum in Philadelphia, the Ninth and Arch Street Museum, about forty miles away from the Pine Barrens. He got his hands on a live kangaroo, painted green stripes on it, attached cardboard wings to its back, and exhibited it at the museum as the Jersey Devil.

In the end, whether people saw the Devil or a deviled kangaroo, some one hundred witnesses across almost a dozen towns and cities saw something strange that week. And Jersey Devil fever has lasted to the present day. Descriptions vary, with witnesses citing everything from the classic winged ram-head to something almost bigfoot-like, but that might be because every monster sighting in New Jersey is attributed to the Devil. That's how powerful it is.

In my own drive through the Pine Barrens, I saw old graffitied ruins, dirt roads lined with roadside crosses, and countless pine trees—but no Devil. Oddly enough, no single town in the Pine Barrens region has made an effort to claim the Devil as its own—not even Leeds Point. I couldn't find a single historical plaque or civic art installation. No museum is dedicated to the legend. The closest things are a Jersey Devil Coaster at a

Six Flags Great Adventure in Jackson Township and the New Jersey Devils NHL team. It's almost as if the state itself is commemoration enough.

But some small businesses have hooked the Devil into their brand, like Lucille's Country Cooking in Barnegat, on the eastern edge of the Pine Barrens. Outside this tiny diner is a large wooden statue of the Devil, with a skull-like head topped by antlers, a brown furry body, red and black wings, and a red barbed tail. It holds a walking stick in its claws. I took a selfie with it and went inside, where I sidled up to the counter and ordered a German omelet and toast (it was too early in the day to dig into the Jersey Devil Burger). Pictures on the wall tipped me off to the Anthony Bourdain connection, and later, when I looked up the 2015 episode of *Parts Unknown* in which the restaurant was featured, I was delighted that they spent a good bit of the segment on the Devil. Bourdain sat at that counter and listened to a local describe the Jersey Devil, to which he replied, "It sounds like My Little Pony with a forked tail. That doesn't sound frightening to me."

◆─────◆─────◆

–International
Cryptozoology Museum –

ROMANTIC ZOOLOGIST

FOUNDER:	CONTENTS:
Loren Coleman	Cryptozoology artifacts;
LOCATION:	life-sized cryptid
Portland, Maine	recreations; pop culture
	ephemera
ESTABLISHED:	
2003	

Would you believe me if I told you that the capital of cryptozoology in the country (and possibly the world) is in . . . Maine? Not in the Bigfootsville that is the Pacific Northwest. Not in Ohio or West Virginia or Wisconsin, all states with a suspiciously wide and varied catalog of monsters. Nope: yellow-slickered and red-lobster'd Maine. A state with a paucity of cryptids, much less famous ones (I mean, specter moose? Wessie the anaconda?). But Maine has something more interesting than a famous cryptid: it has a famous cryptozoologist. And that cryptozoologist has a great museum. The International Cryptozoology Museum is in Portland, Maine, of all the places in the world, simply because that's where Loren Coleman lives.

Coleman, who's in his mid-seventies, has been interested in cryptids for more than sixty years, ever since he watched the 1958 Japanese yeti film *Half-Human*, which fascinated him so deeply that he immediately headed to the local library and discovered the works of some of the founding fathers of cryptozoology: Ivan T. Sanderson, Willy Ley, and Bernard Heuvelmans. These days, it's hard to find a cryptozoology book that doesn't reference him or a cryptozoology documentary that doesn't feature him, regardless of whether it's a work of skepticism or fanaticism. He's found a comfy niche between fringe and fact, caution and crazy, rigor and rebellion. He sees cryptozoology as a subdiscipline of zoology, not a pseudoscience, and not paranormal. He's got no time for that level of weirdness. "I absolutely hate the Fresno Nightcrawler," he told me.

And the International Cryptozoology Museum reflects his personality and interests. Which makes sense, as it all started as a personal collection before he took it public in 2003. The museum features life-size replicas of monsters, casts of bigfoot feet, pop culture ephemera such as cryptid-themed beer cans and action figures, and so much more. "Early criticism of the museum was there are too many toys," he told me. "Toys are part of our culture."

To me, the most interesting artifacts in his collection pertain not to cryptozoology, but to the history of cryptozoology. He has a hair sample found by Sir Edmund Hillary (the first man to summit Mount Everest) during one of his quests to find a yeti in the Himalayas in the 1950s. He has a letter from Jimmy Stewart addressed to him, acknowledging Stewart's role in smuggling a supposed yeti finger bone out of Nepal. Stewart hid it in his wife's lingerie case to get it from India to England. Coleman has artifacts from Tom Slick, Ivan Sanderson, and John Keel, all giants in a field that believes in giants. "I immediately started corresponding with these grandfathers of cryptozoology," he told me. "I sent a letter to any name I found in a book."

At one point, as he toured my family and me around the museum, my kids went crazy over a display dedicated to the Dover Demon, an alien-like creature seen briefly in Massachusetts during the spring of 1977 (see page 58). We had all just watched a documentary on the monster a couple days before. Loren didn't say anything, so I told them, "Loren was the guy who was first on the case. He named the thing." I asked him if he thought the Dover Demon could get a historical plaque like Kentucky's Pascagoula Elephant Men or Maryland's Snarly Yow (page 129 and 44, respectively)—especially since its first sighting was on a still-standing stone wall separating a field from a public road, an easy place for a memorial. "I'd love to do it," he said. "But the problem with the Demon is that some of the more influential residents were upset with me for the name. But it's very famous across the world." He pointed at a Dover Demon figurine on the shelf. "That's from Japan.'"

"So what's changed the most in cryptozoology in your six decades?" I asked. He replied, "Ivan Sanderson told me back in 1965, 'There's only a handful of us in the country.' And he meant like five or ten. When I got involved there were few books, and I was very frustrated by that. Back then cryptozoology was called *romantic zoology*. But that's the first thing. There's more cryptozoologists now and a lot more books." He might have given me a well-deserved side-eye on that one. Whereas I get to go to museums and order books off Amazon to learn about cryptids, he had to drive to gas stations in faraway towns and ask if anything weird had been going on in the area. "Information centers were the worst for that kind of information, but gas stations were great."

"Also, most people are interested in bigfoot these days," he continued. My ears perked up at that observation. Bigfoot has been a thorn in my side throughout this project. Every state seems to have a town that commemorates bigfoot, often over their more interesting local monsters, which is bad news for a book that needs a wide variety of cryptids to work. For instance, Braxton, West Virginia, is home to a famous and unique cryptid called the Flatwoods Monster (page 92) and even has a museum dedicated to it. Yet Braxton also has a bigfoot museum a block away from the Flatwoods Monster Museum. Bigfoot are an invasive species. Coleman said, "They used to be interested in yeti and the Loch Ness Monster, and then all of a sudden, this California notion that there was some hairy creature out there became very popular. People started finding those stories in their backyards."

I pressed him about that universal fascination with bigfoot, leading him with the idea that maybe bigfoot is more believable than other cryptids like, say, a lizard man or a hodag, but he gave me a much more surprising answer: "It's narcissism. People are interested in themselves and what's closest to them. And bigfoot is basically a wild human. People like Mothman because that's scary and people like to be scared. That's why there are horror films. But people would rather talk about bigfoot. When people come in here, and I ask them, 'What's your favorite cryptid?' They almost always say, 'Bigfoot!'"

We wandered the museum, looking at life-sized replicas of creatures such as a tatzelwurm and the Cadborosaurus. There was a Home Depot Halloween prop of a large werewolf. We saw an exhibit on scat and a collection of *Creature from the Black Lagoon* toys. That particular movie monster was inspired by the discovery in 1938 of a living coelacanth, a large fish thought to be extinct for millions of years. The find is often held up by cryptozoologists as proof that undiscovered animals are out there. It's also the logo of the International Cryptozoology Museum.

The collection is special, both for its uniqueness and because it's been assembled through a single person's sensibility. According to Coleman, the museum received 20,000 visitors in 2021. Even though you could throw a rock and hit a bigfoot museum in this country, there's nothing like the International Cryptozoology Museum. Since I interviewed Coleman, he's made news for moving to Bangor, Maine. He's keeping the International Cryptozoology Museum in Portland but opening an adjunct archive to the museum in Bangor, not too far from horror author Stephen King's house.

The last question I asked him was about a statement in his book, *Mysterious America*, originally published in 1983 and updated and reissued in the early 2000s. The statement was, "a cryptozoologist needs to believe nothing but be open to everything." "I still believe that," he said. "I need to hear everyone's stories. If someone says they saw a purple people eater, I want to hear it. Although it doesn't mean that at the end of that process, it needs to go in a case file. When I sign books, I often sign them, 'Enjoy the quest.'"

Jimmy Stewart, Cryptid Smuggler

Legendary actor Jimmy Stewart never starred in a creature feature in his long, acclaimed career, but in real life, the star of Frank Capra's *It's a Wonderful Life* and Alfred Hitchcock's *Rope* found his way into the annals of monsterdom when he smuggled a yeti finger across international borders.

In 1959, Stewart and his wife, Gloria, were visiting India when he received a strange request from a friend, a businessman in the oil industry named Kirk Johnson. Johnson arranged for the Stewarts to meet an associate named Peter Byrne at the Grand Hotel in what was then Calcutta. Byrne had managed to smuggle the mummified finger of what was believed to be a yeti hand from a monastery in Pangboche, Nepal.

No one is sure whether Byrne managed to get his hands on the finger through theft or trade, but, once it was in his own fingers, he was able to walk the relic across the border to India in his backpack. However, he needed to get the finger to London to be examined by a primatologist named William Charles Osman Hill, and customs in India and London were more of a challenge.

That's where Jimmy Stewart comes into the caper. He was at the peak of his fame and could cross country borders with little accosting other than from autograph seekers. The Stewarts agreed, and they secreted the finger in Gloria's underwear case.

The mission was a success. The digit made it to Hill, whose findings vacillated between it being human or inconclusive. The finger then disappeared from the record until 2008, when it was found in a box of the deceased Hill's belongings. It underwent DNA testing that revealed it to be an ordinary human finger, albeit one that had been on an extraordinary journey.

— Snarly Yow —

A BOO WORSE THAN ITS BITE

TYPE:	EARLIEST SIGHTING:
Canine	18th century
LOCATION:	**NOTABLE FEATURE:**
Boonsboro, Maryland	Physical objects pass through it

Snarly Yow. Now that's a proper name for a monster—far scarier and more mysterious than the comic book names of Mothman and Bigfoot. But where the Snarly Yow wins in nomenclature, it possibly loses in nature. The Snarly Yow is a spooky dog—that's it—but a *very* spooky dog. Also known as the Black Dog, this beast mostly guards the main road that cuts through South Mountain, part of the Blue Ridge Mountains in western Maryland, although it's been seen in neighboring parts of West Virginia. Madeleine Vinton Dahlgren, a writer who lived on the mountain, lovingly described the creature in her 1882 book *South-Mountain Magic* as "the dauntless Cerberus of this historic Thermopylæ."

Whatever it is, this Cerberus is no mere stray. Witnesses have described the Snarly Yow as a giant black canine with a vivid red mouth full of sharp teeth. And there seem to have been a wide range of witnesses over the past couple hundred years, from pioneers, preachers, hunters, and farmers all the way up to modern-day Sunday drivers on what is now Alternate

Route 40. In 1975, according to the book *Haunted Houses of Harpers Ferry* by Stephen D. Brown, a thirty-year-old man by the name of William was taking a walk when he saw a black dog, bigger than any dog he had ever seen, step onto the road. He tried to scare it away by throwing rocks and sticks at it, but they passed through the creature like it was made of fog. In 1976, as reported in a 1989 article in the *Washington Post*, a local couple hit what they thought was a large blue-black dog with glowing eyes with their car. When they got out to look, there was nothing in the road. Not even a bloodstain on the ground or a tuft of hair in their car grill.

The Snarly Yow seems to be mutable, vanishing or growing bigger or changing the color of its coat (one witness saw its black fur sprout white spots). Fists, bullets, cars—nothing seems able to touch it. Sometimes the Snarly Yow is seen crossing the road to the nearby stream. Other times it stands ominously in the middle of the road, although it seems to be more a reminder of the terrors and wonders of the world than a threat. In the hundreds of years of encounters with the Snarly Yow, not a single attack has been recorded. The only associated injury was the broken collarbone of a man who attempted to chase the Snarly Yow down on a horse that did not at all agree with that decision. The debate is ongoing over whether the hellhound prowling South Mountain is a ghost or a cryptid—or the ghost of a cryptid. Certainly, it haunts the area like a ghost. Or perhaps it's merely being

territorial like any other canine.

There have been enough reports of this American Hound of the Baskervilles to set its claws deeply into the psyche of the region, a psyche already scarred by a history of violence, from numerous battles spanning colonial times to the Revolutionary War and the Civil War. Today, those battlefields have been preserved. And wherever there's a preserved battlefield, there is a historic placard. Across the street from the Old South Mountain Inn in Boonsboro (built in 1732) are half a dozen placards set together in a small field. They tell various stories about the mountain itself, the people who explored it, and the vicious battles that pocked the land with both cannonball craters and graves.

One of those placards covers the history of the national road that cuts through the mountain: Alternate Route 40. It was the first federally funded road in the nation and linked Baltimore, Maryland, to Vandalia, Illinois. Little did they know they were paving through monster territory. A sidebar depicts the silhouette of a scraggly canine howling at the moon above the title BEWARE OF THE SNARLY YOW. The single paragraph of explanation centers on an encounter in which a hunter spied the creature and shot at it multiple times. The bullets seemed to pass right through the Snarly Yow without any effect, as if the hunter was shooting at a shadow. The story ends with the poetic "Finally, overcome with dread, the huntsman fled."

It's a small memorial to a minor creature in cryptid lore. But it's still more than many cryptids get. And maybe the creature isn't quite Snarly Yow Festival–worthy—but you never know until you try.

– Snallygaster –

DEAD DRUNK DEMON DRAGON

TYPE:	EARLIEST SIGHTING:
Aerial	1909
LOCATION:	**NOTABLE FEATURE:**
Western Maryland	Beak full of tentacles

The Snallygaster looks like a chicken crossed with a dragon choking on an octopus. It has wings, claws, a sharp beak full of tentacles, either one eye or three, and a long tail. It likes to eat people. It may have died a long time ago, dissolved in a vat of moonshine.

It's a difficult creature to imagine, that Snallygaster, but if you ever find yourself in Sykesville, Maryland, just outside Baltimore, you don't have to. In 2018, the town installed a scavenger hunt of ten small murals in the alleyways and on the buildings of the town's Main Street. Each painting is by a different artist. In one mural, a pair of girls encounters a small, fairy-winged reptile. In another, a full-grown, tentacle-bearded monster swoops over a flooded town. Yet another gives the Snallygaster a Hawaiian shirt and Elvis hair. Each painting depicts a scene from a fictional tale called *The Curse of the Snallygaster*, written by a local museum curator named Jack White.

The real story of the Snallygaster starts centuries before, further west, in Maryland's Frederick and Washington counties, where German immigrants brought the legend of a

reptile-bird called the *Schneller Geist* ("fast ghost") with them. They even hung stars called hex signs on their barns to protect themselves from it and other monstrous misfortunes, stars that you can still see today on barns in the area. According to local legends, over the centuries, the Snallygaster's train whistle of a screech could be heard echoing among the mountains and valleys. And that's if you were lucky. If you were unlucky, it would attack you, either draining your blood or eating you in gruesome chunks with its sharp beak and teeth and tentacles.

But it wasn't until 1909 that the creature firmly planted its talons in Maryland lore, at around the same time that the Jersey Devil was spotted further north (see page 33). Some speculate witnesses may have even seen the same creature. Reports poured in of a winged beast flying around South Mountain (the same mountain haunted by the Snarly Yow—see page 44) and attacking people. In one report, the Snallygaster plucked one man from the ground, flew to the top of a hill, and punctured his jugular with its beak. In another, a hunter took a shot at it as it flew overhead, but the bullet merely caromed off its hide and enraged it. The hunter escaped by jumping into a stable. The Snallygaster was even supposed to have laid eggs near the towns of Burkittesville and Gapland. Eventually both the flurry of articles and the flap of its wings faded from the worries of western Maryland.

In 1932, it lanced the air of the region again, terrorizing the populace anew with death and dismemberment from above. But then, mere weeks after its reemergence in the media, the *Middletown Valley Register* announced that the Snallygaster had died. According to the story, it was drawn to Frog Hollow in Washington County by the fumes of a 2,500-gallon vat of moonshine. The fumes were too much for it, though, and wilted the creature out of the air and directly into the boiling, lye-filled mash, dissolving it to bones. The moonshiners ran away, afraid the commotion would draw the authorities, which it did. Prohibition officers George T. Danforth and Charles E. Cushwa were soon on the scene. "Imagine our feeling when our eyes feasted on the monster submerged in the liquor vat," said Danforth to the paper. A monster wasn't going to keep them from their duty to dry up the county, though, so they laced the place with 560 pounds of dynamite and blew everything to legend.

Today, in Frederick, Maryland, somebody is trying to resurrect the Snallygaster. I met Sarah Cooper at a pizzeria in downtown Frederick. She's an ER nurse from Texas who has lived in Maryland for more than a decade. At some point she not only became obsessed with the story of the Snallygaster, she became its PR agent. She immediately inundated me with Snallygaster materials—T-shirts, art, newspaper clippings, toys, and books. "A lot of people have said to me, 'I've heard that name before, but I didn't know what it was,'" she said. "I would love for Frederick to embrace it."

Currently, the only traces of the Snallygaster in Frederick are the Snallygaster's Exploratorium, which is the children's library of the local historical society museum; a themed flavor at an ice cream shop downtown; and a limited edition Snallygaster Whisky offered by a local distiller. Cooper plans on filling that hole in the monster map by creating her own museum, the American Snallygaster Museum. When I spoke to her in August 2021, her plan was to erect a custom barn within the next eight months on her property in Libertytown, just outside of Frederick, and fill that barn with art, pop culture artifacts, and newspaper clippings. Hopefully she'll hang a hex sign on it.

"What's your big photo op?" I asked. Every monster museum

needs a signature photo op, whether it's the giant, furry Crookston Bigfoot at the International Cryptozoology Museum in Maine or the life-sized Flatwoods Monster at the Flatwoods Monster Museum in West Virginia. "A big Snallygaster that looks like it's been taxidermied," she answered. "The museum is going to have the vibe of the Mystery Shack from *Gravity Falls*," she said, referencing an animated Disney series about monsters and mysteries. Cooper has a bigger vision that goes beyond even the Snallygaster. She wants to grow the museum into one dedicated to all Maryland monsters, including the Snarly Yow (Marylanders sure do know how to name their monsters). "I want to make Maryland magical. We have all this magical stuff and we're not talking about it."

And then she told me about the dark side of the Snallygaster, a dark side that several cryptids likely share and one which she wants to make sure is not ignored at her museum. "The Snallygaster was sometimes used to scare people of color, either enslaved people from escaping or freed people of color from voting." She showed me a photocopy of a 1909 article in the *Middletown Valley Register* about the Snallygaster that bore the headline THE COLORED PEOPLE ARE IN GREAT DANGER. The subhead was: ATTACKS ONLY COLORED MEN.

With the Snallygaster still being a relatively obscure cryptid, Cooper will have a huge influence over the monster's brand with her museum, both the good aspects of it and the bad. And something tells me it won't stop at a small museum on her personal property. "I really don't understand why nobody else here has been this crazy about the Snallygaster," she said. "Why don't we have a Snallygaster festival? We have such cool places in Frederick to do it." I couldn't agree more.

– Gloucester Sea Serpent –

THE PERFECT WYRM

TYPE:	EARLIEST SIGHTING:
Aquatic	1817
LOCATION:	**SIZE:**
Gloucester, Massachusetts	60–100 feet long, 3 feet thick

The Gloucester Sea Serpent is the most well-docu-mented cryptid in history. Its appearance was no brief splash and blurry picture. No, this sea serpent boldly displayed itself for two whole years off the coast of Cape Ann in Massachusetts. In that time, it was seen by thousands of people, both from the shores of Gloucester and in the water. It was studied by scientists and attacked by sailors. Crowds numbering in the hundreds watched it cavort in the waves for hours. Its fame spanned the ocean, with Europeans calling it the Great American Sea Serpent. Writer and podcaster Rob Morphy described it on the site Cryptopia as "one of the most scientifically respected encounters in the annals of cryptozoology, and ... one of the great unsolved mysteries of the sea."

And yet, nobody has bothered to give it an affectionate nickname like its freshwater cousins: Nessie, Chessie, Bessie, and Tahoe Tessie, to name a few examples. That might be because the diminutive "Gloustie" sounds awful, like one of the negative side effects of a pharmaceutical. Nevertheless, the

Gloucester Sea Serpent truly earned its place among the greats. The magic began in August 1817, when a long humpy thing was found swimming around the cape. It had a flattened, serpentine head as big as a horse; was somewhere between sixty and one hundred feet long, three feet thick, dark in color; and had a four-foot-long tongue. In other words, a classic sea serpent.

Over the span of 1817 to 1819, the serpent starred in a long-running game of cat-and-mouse. Sailors reportedly shot it in the head twice at close range, but the musket balls bounced off harmlessly. A harpoon tossed at it was similarly ineffective. Landlubbers searched for monster eggs on shore. It was sighted so often in this city of salt-seasoned fishers that people thought catching it was inevitable—so inevitable that a shed was pre-emptively built near Faneuil Hall in Boston to house its carcass. Writer Ben Shattuck phrased it best when he wrote in a *Salon* article that "this 'serpent' was in their harbor, right under their noses—something equivalent to a Sasquatch walking across the parking lot of a hunting expo."

The Linnaean Society of New England, a proto-scientific society, interviewed witnesses and published an illustrated paper on Gloustie. At one point a lumpy, four-foot-long snake was found on land and delivered to the society. They deemed it to be the sea serpent's offspring and dubbed the species *Scoliophis atlanticus*. Further analysis revealed that the smaller creature was merely a deformed snake. Still, through all of that, the Gloucester Sea Serpent kept undulating. And in those two years, although nobody could catch it, nobody could debunk it, either. Eventually, like some feral cat you feed from your back porch until one day it doesn't show up, Gloustie's snake head submerged forever.

You might think such a landmark event would be

city-shaping, but for over a century the only sign that a scaly monster had once terrorized Gloucester was a mural of a green reptile on a boulder at Cressy Beach. Painted in 1955 by nineteen-year-old local artist Robert Stephenson, the serpent looks more medieval than aquatic and, according to one resident who knew him (Stephenson died in 2015), Stephenson meant it to evoke Quetzalcoatl, the Mesoamerican dragon-like deity, and not Gloustie. Still, most residents associate the mural with the serpent.

However, the Gloucester Sea Serpent recently, finally received its proper due outside Gloucester's Cape Ann Museum just one and a half miles from Cressy Beach. In 2017, on the 200th anniversary of that first 1817 sighting, the museum unveiled a magnificent bronze statue of the Gloucester Sea Serpent wrapped around a rock. Created by artist Chris Williams, the statue is smaller and thinner than the creature's traditional size estimate (although it still rears up nine feet tall), but makes up for the scale with its unabashed, terrifying monstrousness. Its toothy mouth and soulless eyes will take you right to the bottom of the cold, dark Gloucester Harbor.

Once you have a large statue of your monster set in a prominent place downtown, you've leveled up your Cryptid Town status. All Gloucester needs to do is wrap another sea serpent around its famous Fisherman's Memorial, and the city will start to approach Loch Ness levels of local pride for Gloustie (if gloustiness persists longer than six hours, please see your doctor).

– Puckwudgie –

PORCUPINE PEOPLE OF
BRIDGEWATER TRIANGLE

TYPE:	EARLIEST SIGHTING:
Humanoid	Prehistory
LOCATION:	**SIZE:**
Bridgewater Triangle, Massachusetts	2–4 feet tall

Massachusetts has its own version of the Bermuda Tri-angle. You can find it, if you dare, in the southeast part of the state, west of Cape Cod. It's called the Bridgewater Triangle. According to cryptozoologist Loren Coleman, who named and demarcated the area in the 1970s, its three points are the towns of Abington, Rehoboth, and Freetown. The triangle encompasses Hockomock Swamp, one of the largest swamps in New England, as well as the Freetown State Forest and the city of Taunton. The Bridgewater Triangle is supposed to be a wild place full of high strangeness and terror. Ghosts haunt its roads and marshes and forests. UFOs streak its skies. A few cryptids call the triangle home—bigfoot, of course, and thunderbirds. Puckwudgies fit right into that bizarre melee.

Puckwudgies (also spelled pukwudgies or pukwudgees) range in height from two to four feet, with oversized human facial features and a thick bush of quills or bristles sprouting from their backs and heads. From behind, they look like porcupines standing on their back legs. Puckwudgies are often depicted as wearing simple clothing and carrying small bows notched with poison-tipped arrows. Some stories go so far as to imbue them with magical abilities. They can turn invisible or shapeshift, control fire, and cloud people's minds. Puckwudgie has been translated variously from different Native American languages as "person of the forest," "little wild man of the forest," "little people," and "little people who disappear."

These creatures are humanoid and intelligent, like the Menehune of Hawaii (page 241) and the gnomes of Minnesota (page 199) and the various aliens invading this book. Stories of puckwudgies can be found throughout the Great Lakes and New England. In Massachusetts, these cryptid-beings originate from Wampanoag lore, which describes the creatures as being mostly minor nuisances until people attempted to either expel or exterminate them by enlisting the help of Maushop, the giant who created Cape Cod. The attempt failed, and the puckwudgies became angry and malevolent. Henry Wadsworth Longfellow, who lived in Massachusetts, included puckwudgies in his 1855 epic poem *The Song of Hiawatha*, in which the creatures try to kill Kwasind, one of Hiawatha's friends.

These days, the creatures are essentially viewed as gremlins. They are responsible for everything from minor mischief to murder. One of their most notorious practices is to cause brain fog in their victims and lure them to their deaths over cliffs. Assonet Ledge in Freetown is often pointed to as a favorite murder spot for puckwudgies, although the deaths are classified as suicides or accidents because the coroner doesn't have a puckwudgie tick box on their autopsy form.

In 2017, local police in Freetown affixed PUKWUDGIE XING signs near the entrance to Freetown State Forest on Slab Bridge

Road. It was an attempt to get motorists to slow down because the number of animal collisions on the road was rising. The police believed that yet another of the ubiquitous deer-crossing signs wouldn't generate so much as a tap on the brakes, but that people would definitely slow down for a double-take when they saw the evil-looking, spiky-backed creature on the diamond-shaped sign. It was a temporary gesture, one timed with April Fool's Day, but the idea of permanent puckwudgie signs installed throughout the area, in addition to being a helpful safety measure, could be a nice little tourism lift for the area.

The signs could also serve as a warning—and not just for motorists. Because if you ever find yourself in the Bridgewater Triangle, in between hiding from abducting aliens and dodging ghostly hitchhikers, you should be especially wary of any porcupines you see. And stay far away from cliffs

– Dover Demon –

A YOUNG ADULT HORROR STORY

TYPE:	EARLIEST SIGHTING:
Alien	1977
LOCATION:	SIZE:
Dover, Massachusetts	3–4 feet tall

The Dover Demon was a two-night-only show, but what a pair of nights. It involves pot-smoking teenagers, a SWAT team of paranormal researchers, and a unique-enough critter—somewhere between alien and animal—to expand the boundaries of cryptid-kind. That plus the spooky eyewitness drawings go a long way toward bumping this guy to the upper edge of the cryptid B-team, ready to be called to the majors as soon as we bore of bigfoot or Mothman.

On the night of April 21, 1977, three teenagers were driving down Farm Street in the Boston suburb of Dover. On one side of the dark road were houses, on the other a short stone fence separating the road from an empty field. The driver of the car, William Bartlett, spotted a strange creature scrabbling on all fours atop the stone fence. According to the book *Mysterious America*, he described it to both police and private investigators as three or four feet tall, half of which was its large, watermelon-shaped head. Its body was like "a baby's body with long arms and legs," its color was bright peach like "Fred Flintstone in the Sunday comics," and it looked to have a texture like wet sandpaper. It sported no discernable mouth or nose or ears, but it had glowing orange eyes. Its hands and feet had long digits that wrapped around the stones on the wall. Bartlett would later admit to a few puffs of the magic dragon that night, but not a hallucinate-a-weird-monster amount. No one else in the car witnessed the creature. Bartlett went home and drew up an iconic sketch of what he saw, which has become one of the most recognizable sketches in cryptozoology.

Two hours later (now April 22) and about a mile away from the first sighting, another teenager was walking home on Miller Hill Road, which intersects with Farm Street. His name was John Baxter. He saw a diminutive figure coming toward him. Thinking it was a kid he knew, he called out to him. The figure didn't respond. When they were fifteen feet away from each other, Baxter realized the thing wasn't human. It ran off on two legs, and Baxter pursued it for a few steps before reconsidering. The creature stopped briefly on a rock, and Baxter saw its long toes wrap around the rock and its upper limbs wrap around a tree. Its eyes glowed. Baxter ran away, hitched a ride home, and would go on to draw another tattoo-worthy image that closely matched Bartlett's.

The next night (still April 22), two more teenagers, Abby Brabham and Will Tainter, were driving around Dover when they saw a creature in an adjoining field on Springdale Avenue, which also connects to Farm Street. Only Brabham got a good look at the creature, describing it as a hairless tan monkey with an oblong head. Its eyes glowed green.

All of these sightings occurred in a little more than twenty-four hours across a stretch of two miles of Dover—and then nobody ever saw the Dover Demon again. It became a story passed around the halls of Dover's high school, destined to be forgotten when *Star Wars* debuted a month later. Except that Loren Coleman needed bread and milk.

The cryptid expert lived in the next town over from Dover. About a week after the encounters, he happened to be in the Dover Country Store when he saw a sketch of the creature that somebody had taped up inside the shop. He inquired about it, and then immediately began investigating the case. After interviewing the witnesses, he brought in Joseph Nyman, Ed Fogg, and Walter Webb, all of whom were members of various UFO organizations and lived in nearby towns. Webb was also assistant director of the Hayden Planetarium at the Boston Science Museum. Coleman had no reason to suspect that the creature was from the stars, but he knew that Webb's scientific mind would come in handy.

The team of Fox Mulders reinterviewed the witnesses, checked weather reports, talked to the police, interviewed parents and teachers and other character references, visited the sites, reenacted the encounters, circulated the drawings, and in general gave more attention to the case in the direct wake of the sighting than perhaps any other cryptid has received. Coleman himself was the one to dub the creature the Dover Demon.

The investigators finished their report in September of that year, unfazed by the debut of *Star Wars*. Their report, which was written by Webb, concluded:

> *The Dover Demon is a disturbing, bizarre affair. There are many frustrating, troublesome aspects about it. . . . It is without apparent precedent. But despite the doubts and questions this episode raises, I believe a hoax is unlikely and the report should be classified as a low-weight unknown.*

Today, almost half a century later, that area of Dover is virtually unchanged—large houses, low stone fences, open fields, forest. Although I could suggest one small change: a plaque dedicated to the Dover Demon affixed to that classic New England stone fence that still lines Farm Road on which it was first seen.

Ufology and Cryptozoology: Weirdos Unite

You're out in the forest looking for bigfoot, hooting out your best bigfoot call, attempting to lure it with Milky Way bars (they like sweets). Instead of a giant hairy beast, though, a flying saucer appears in front of you. Are you disappointed? Of course not. Because cryptozoology and ufology go together like nougat and caramel.

Cryptozoologists and ufologists both believe that reality is slightly-to-vastly different from what is commonly accepted. Both groups believe that first contact with aliens and cryptids has already been made. Both groups' beliefs are criticized as being pseudoscience. They have to stand staunch against skepticism while sorting through frustratingly little physical evidence.

Ufology and cryptozoology both deal with monsters and mysteries—and the mystery aspect can blur the lines between them. In a sense, aliens *are* cryptids: creatures that have been witnessed but not verified by science. It goes the other way, too. Sometimes cryptids are explained as possible alien visitors, like the Loveland Frogman or the Dover Demon.

Often when there is a flurry of cryptid sightings, it's accompanied by a simultaneous flurry of UFO sightings. The Whitehall bigfoot sighting kicked off a week full of both giant furry things on the ground and giant glowing things in the sky. So it went the year that Mothman terrorized Point Pleasant.

Cryptid fans and alien fans have a lot to discuss and even more to commiserate over at the local bar after a long night of watching the skies and camping in the forests. And they do it right alongside the paranormalists, who have spent their own long nights in abandoned mansions looking for ghosts. Where is this bar? I want to hang out with them all.

– Albatwitch –

AN APPLE A DAY KEEPS THE MONSTERS AT BAY

TYPE:	EARLIEST SIGHTING:
Humanoid	19th century
LOCATION:	**SIZE:**
Columbia, Pennsylvania	4 feet tall

Chickies Rock in Lancaster County, Pennsylvania, can be a dangerous place. At least a dozen people have died falling from its edge, down the one hundred feet of its vertiginous face. Also, you have to watch out for the albatwitches while you're there—especially if you're carrying apples.

Albatwitches are what serious cryptozoologists call "hairy hominids," and what not-quite-as-serious ones call "little bigfeet." They're four-foot-tall, thin, hairy, primate-like creatures—kid cousins to the giant sasquatches, shooting guards on the bigfoot basketball team. Their name is traditionally understood to be a Pennsylvania Dutch corruption of the phrase "apple-snitches" because the creatures love to steal apples.

There's uncertainty about whether the albatwitch derives from the lore of the native Susquehannock peoples, or the immigrant Pennsylvania Dutch, or if its legend evolved much more recently. We do know that as early as the 1920s, albatwitches were part of a specific practical joke known as a snipe hunt in other areas of the country. Groups would take a victim out into the woods, hand them a bag, and then ostensibly go out and beat the bushes to chase an albatwitch toward the bag-holder so that they could catch the creature. Of course, that's not what happened. The bush-beaters just left their victim alone in the woods while they all went home or to the local tavern to wait until the lonely albatwitch hunter realized that they had been duped into hunting a fictitious creature.

But, unlike snipes, there have been actual sightings of albatwitches in Lancaster County. The ape-like beings have been spotted running across roads or through the forest or swinging along the tops of trees. There are stories of albatwitches pelting picnickers with apple cores after stealing their apples. In the documentary series *Legends of Lancaster*, Chris Vera, the director of the Columbia Historic Preservation Society, tells the story of a childhood friend of his playing hide and seek in the woods when an albatwitch pinned him to a tree with its arms. His friend screamed, and the albatwitch ran away. Vera also remembers a local cemetery, Laurel Hill Memorial Gardens, being closed by the police when somebody spotted a dark, hairy humanoid wandering around inside.

The main habitat of the albatwitches is the area around Chickies Rock at Chickies Rock County Park. Chickies Rock (from the Lenape word *Chiquesalunga*, or "place of crayfish") is an outcropping of quartzite at the western end of Chickies Ridge. It rises 100 feet above the Susquehanna River, and its summit is accessible by an easy mile of trail. Directly beneath it is a biking path and railroad tracks, while across the river you can see into the next county, York, as well as the town of Marietta. On my hike, I didn't see a single reference to the creatures. No BEWARE OF ALBATWITCHES or APPLES NOT PERMITTED signs anywhere. It's almost like they want you to get pegged in the head by an apple core thrown from the trees.

However, the albatwitches *are* commemorated in the nearby town of Columbia—for one day a year, at least. Columbia has hosted an annual Albatwitch Day since 2014. The festival features music and paranormal lectures, trolley tours to Chickies Rock (where you can throw apples into the woods to feed the albatwitches), and, of course, plenty of albatwitch merch. It also showcases a multitude of apple-themed dishes and sweets. Albatwitches are one of the few—possibly only—cryptids associated with a particular food. Just adding apple is enough to create an albatwitch-themed dish.

But I think more can be done for the albatwitch. Since hairy hominids rule the cryptid zoo, and since albatwitches have a way cooler name than bigfoot, I think the albatwitch should have more than just its day. I personally want a DO NOT FEED THE ALBATWITCHES sign at Chickies Rock.

– Glawackus –

THE WACKY CAT-DOG OF GLASTONBURY

TYPE:	EARLIEST SIGHTING:
Mammalian	1939
LOCATION:	SIZE:
Glastonbury, Connecticut	4 feet long

It's a dog! It's a cat! No, it's the Glawackus of Glaston-bury, Connecticut. Which is possibly a dog *and* a cat—or a bear. It's confusing.

The Glawackus story is a rare one in that everybody in town had fun with the creature sighting right away. Cryptid stories usually start out as horror tales, all glowing eyes and terrifying screams in the night, panicked phone calls to the police who immediately query if the caller is drunk or high. Then comes the post-commotion embarrassment of becoming one of "those places," a town frightened by a creature that is not supposed to exist. But finally the story ends happily decades later with acceptance, cryptid capitalization, and pride. (Or, alternately, economic despair, cryptid capitalization, and pride.) However, the Glawackus united Glastonbury immediately.

Something dark and monstrous started attacking livestock and pets in the sleepy town of Glastonbury in January 1939. But as the witness reports poured in, they sounded like they were all touching different parts of the elephant with their eyes closed. The creature was described variously as a panther, a bear, a lynx, a lion, and a big dog. One person described it as having tusks. Another said that it looked like a cat up front and a dog in the back. Yet another claimed that it looked like a dog up front but a cat in the back. It was even said, possibly in jest, that the Glawackus was a blue wolverine whose eyes leaked blue tears. If you conduct a Google image search of the Glawackus today, you'll see plenty of artist renditions of the beast, while coming away without any firm image in your mind.

Even though nobody knew what the Glawackus really looked like, the people of Glastonbury sure had a blast with it. Hunting parties were organized (emphasis on *parties*). The monster hunters tromped through snowy forests and posed for newspaper photos, guns drawn. The town threw Glawackus dances in honor of the beast (anybody bearing a real Glawackus would be allowed in free). The *Hartford Courant* had its best run ever, concocting howling headlines (GUFFAWS OF GLASTONBURY GLAWACKUS GREET GLOOMY GANG OF GUNNERS), running satires, and selling Glawackus-themed ads. One issue featured a full-page spread of those ads centered around an artist's conception that looks like a lion with a unicorn horn jutting from its head. A local furrier promised, WE WILL GLADLY TAKE THE GLAWACKUS PELT AND MAKE A COAT OR SCARF AT OUR REGULAR RATES. A local salon admonished, DON'T LOOK LIKE A GLAWACKUS. A market warned, WE CAN'T AGREE TO SUPPLY YOU WITH GLAWACKUS STEAKS. A service station cautioned, BE READY FOR A QUICK GETAWAY FROM THE GLASTONBURY GLAWACKUS. The *Hartford Courant* was even responsible for the creature's delightful name. One of its editors, Frank King, put together the words *Glastonbury* and *wacky* and tacked on a Latin-sounding *-us* to give it gravitas. The achievement earned a line in his obituary.

After a few months, a run of national headlines, and hundreds of empty-handed hunters, Glawackus fever died down. The creature would be spotted a couple of times in the 1950s and 1960s, but it never caught on again like it did in those frosty days of early 1939. It seems strange to feel nostalgic about the time a town was besieged by a monster, but the story of the Glawackus in Glastonbury makes it sound like a blast.

Today, it's not celebrated anymore. But it should be—even if they can't figure out how to draw it for the festival T-shirts.

Prime Hook
Swamp Creature

A TWENTY-FIRST-CENTURY CRYPTID

TYPE:	EARLIEST SIGHTING:
Mammalian	2007
LOCATION:	SIZE:
Milton, Delaware	2.5–3 feet tall

Most tales of cryptids reach back decades or centuries, long enough ago that sometimes the original sighting is lost to time or lacks important details. In Delaware, we have the opportunity to get in on the ground floor of a new cryptid. It's called the Prime Hook Swamp Creature, and it might be the most darling cryptid since the jackalope. Also, I'm sort of forced to go in this direction because Delaware, as the second tiniest state in the union—barely a cleft of Maryland—is so small it records almost no cryptid sightings. Other than Bigfoot—he's everywhere. But this book isn't *The United States of Bigfoot*.

Prime Hook is a national wildlife preserve on the Delaware Bay, north of Lewes. Its 10,000 acres of Delaware wetlands are home to hundreds of known animal species—including migratory birds, horseshoe crabs, bald eagles, fox squirrels—and maybe one unknown animal species.

Around 2010, three meager paragraphs credited to a "Helen J." were posted to the paranormal section of About.com, the now-defunct precursor to Wikipedia. Helen stated that she and her daughter—whose age is unrecorded—were driving Broadkill Road at the edge of Prime Hook one day in July 2007 when they saw a strange creature on the side of the road. She described it as "2½ to 3 feet tall with long legs, a tan body, a flat, almost puggish face, and a long tail. It had small ears and looked to be about 30 pounds." She wasn't clear in her description whether it walked on two or four legs. According to Helen's account, it wasn't the first time that her family had come across the creature, either. About a year previously, her other daughter and her friend had been driving in that same area at night when a similar pug-fox-like thing ran across the road in front of their car.

Helen was curious enough about the creature that she went off to find a local to ask about it. She visited what she called the Prime Hook Reserve museum (possibly the Prime Hook National Wildlife Refuge Visitor Contact Station in Milton), but the staff there couldn't help her. She eventually talked to a woman who owned what Helen called the Broadkill Beach store, which is probably the Broadkill Store, a seasonal gift shop and eatery that's been on Broadkill Beach for more than a century. The store owner admitted to seeing a creature that fit Helen's description years before while out dirt biking with her father. Helen ended her account with, "I am wondering if anyone else has seen it and what the heck it is."

That's it. That's the whole story. So innocuous a sighting and so mundane a creature as to be completely believable. But this is how cryptid stories begin and promulgate in the digital era. Every cryptid starts with one sighting, after all.

Helen's story was part of a larger About.com project that gathered monster sightings from individual submitters.

However, of all the monsters documented there, it's the Prime Hook Swamp Creature that seems to get the most (if still minimal) traction more than a decade later. Artists have tried their hand at depicting it, the story has been reposted to other forums, and a few cryptid researchers have begun digging into it for blog, podcast, and, ahem, book fodder. The original (and only recorded) story of the creature has already begun to mutate in the telling. I've seen one writer ascribe a mane to it, even though that's not in the original post. Eventually—hopefully—stories of the Prime Hook Swamp Creature will snowball until it has crab claws, a prehensile tail, and its own festival.

Or maybe not. The biggest issue with the Prime Hook Swamp Creature is not the fact that its story springs from a single, brief anonymous testimony—that's often the case with cryptids. The issue is that it's a cute, pug-like, seemingly nonthreatening cryptid. Cryptozoology rarely elevates cute cryptids. It's more focused on monsters with glowing eyes that cause entire towns of people to quake in their boots. But the animal kingdom has plenty of cute animals in its taxonomy, so I figure cryptozoology should, too. Plus, a cute cryptid could be a boon for, say, a certain Broadkill Beach store involved in the story to adopt as a mascot and start printing on T-shirts.

– Glocester Ghoul –

HERE BE MONSTERS (AND PIRATES)

TYPE:	EARLIEST SIGHTING:
Reptilian	1839
LOCATION:	**NOTABLE FEATURE:**
Glocester, Rhode Island	Fire-breathing

There aren't many dragon-like cryptids in the US. There are plenty of reptilian cryptids, but few fire-breathing, scaly beasts with wings—which seems strange, given that dragons are omnipresent in mythologies and cultures across the world. But Rhode Island has us covered; The smallest state in the country boasts a dragon cryptid, and we might be able to thank a pirate (or two) for that.

Albert Hicks was more than just a pirate. He was an early template for the New York gangster, a cold-blooded career criminal who committed a lot of his murder and theft while at sea. His final crime was the brutal murder of three men on a boat in New York Harbor, and his life ended like so many other pirates' had: dangling from a knotted loop of rope. In fact, he was one of the last people ever executed for piracy in the United States. He was hanged on July 13, 1860, on what was then Bedloe Island, just off the southern tip of Manhattan. Today, we call it Liberty Island, and its defining feature is a giant, mint-green statue of a crowned woman bearing a torch. But even though Hicks's story ended in New York, it began in Rhode Island. And it involves not only a dragon, but a pirate treasure.

Hicks was born in Foster, Rhode Island. According to his death row autobiography, he loved listening to stories about pirates when he was a child and fantasized about finding their treasures, some of which were rumored to have been buried in the farmlands around his hometown. It was reported in the *Boston Globe* thirty-six years after his death that he went looking for this treasure—specifically, the treasure of the infamous Captain Kidd, the Scottish pirate hanged in London whose legendary treasure hordes buried on the Atlantic Coast of North America inspired Robert Louis Stevenson's *Treasure Island.* Hicks heard that Kidd's Spanish doubloons had been found at a farm in nearby Glocester, so he and three of his cronies—John Jepp, Ben Cobb, and Ben Saunders—snuck onto the farm one night with their lanterns and shovels.

Instead of treasure, they discovered the monster that would come to be known as the Glocester Ghoul. The newspaper account includes a detailed description of the beast credited to Hicks, although it's unsourced and doesn't appear in his autobiography:

> It was a large animal, with staring eyes as big as pewter bowls. The eyes looked like balls of fire. When it breathed as it went by, flames came out of its mouth and nostrils, scorching the brush in its path. It was as a big as a cow with dark wings on each side like a bat's. It had spiral horns like a ram's, as big around as a stovepipe. Its feet were formed like a duck's and measured a foot and a half across. The body was covered with scales as big as clamshells, which made a rattling noise as the beast moved along. The scales flopped up and down. The thing had lights on its sides like those shining through a tin lantern.

I was raised on enough *Scooby-Doo* episodes to know that where there's treasure to be found, somebody is dressing up like a monster to keep people away from it. And this description of the Glocester Ghoul sounds that way with its rattling noises, floppy scales, and lantern-like lights. Hicks and his companions didn't have time to do any unmasking, though. According to the account, the monster "seemed to come from nowhere and to go away in the same manner." They fled without finding any treasure.

But fifty-seven years later, the monster returned. In January 1896, Glocester resident Neil Hopkins was traveling home when he was chased through the cold night by a monster that sounds a lot like the one from Hicks's account. According to the *Boston Globe*, Hopkins described it as such: "It seemed to be all a-fire; it had a hot breath. There was a metallic sound, like the clanking of steel against steel." He described it as the size of elephant, and with no tail. It chased him for a short distance before disappearing into the forest.

The final mystery is why the beast was dubbed the Glocester Ghoul instead of the Glocester Dragon, but I guess that's to be expected from the people who named their non-island state Rhode Island. Regardless, the ghoul is a big monster that the smallest state in the union should be making a much bigger deal out of.

–Derry Fairy–

A CHRISTMAS CRYPTID

TYPE:	EARLIEST SIGHTING:
Alien	1967
LOCATION:	**SIZE:**
Derry, New Hampshire	2 feet tall

New Hampshire is somewhat bereft when it comes to cryptids. It's a small state, sure, but it's also a state that is 81 percent covered by forest. You should be able to hide something in all that woodland. In the cryptid encyclopedias and online listicles, you'll find lip service to a few New Hampshire cryptids, but they're all skimpy on the details. New Hampshire is supposed to host Wood Devils (skinny bigfoot), Devil Monkeys (monkeys), and a Dublin Lake Monster (which is so vague we don't even know its shape). I can see why New Hampshire bets its tourism investments on extraterrestrials instead. It was, after all, the site of the first and most influential alien abduction in modern times (Betty and Barney Hill's), as well as one of the more well-documented UFO flyovers, the Exeter Incident. It has commemorated those weird encounters with historic placards, exhibits, and festivals. So I think if New Hampshire had a cryptid worth commemorating, it probably would.

And maybe it does. I'd vote for the Derry Fairy: because its name rhymes, because no other state is known for its fairies, and because it's a Christmas cryptid. The country is ravenous for Christmas monsters. All we really have is Krampus, which we imported from the Alpine region of Europe, and we're beating that yuletide beast into the snow-covered ground. Let's get to the story.

In December 1956, Alfred Horne, who was in his mid-seventies, went out into the woods of his property on Berry Road in Derry to cut down a Christmas tree. But instead of the perfect evergreen tree, he came across a strange, small, green creature. It was two feet tall, with a domed head, filmy eyes, droopy ears, and no digits on its stubby limbs. Its flesh was loose and elephantine. You may be thinking the Derry Fairy's not exactly Tinkerbell, but *fairy* is a catch-all term that includes goblins and gnomes and trolls and other similar creatures. Plus, you can't say no to a good rhyme.

Both Horne and the fairy froze when they saw each other. As the minutes passed, Horne realized that he was at a crossroads. If he ran away and told his story, he'd be called crazy. If he could actually catch the thing, fame and fortune were sure to follow. So he tried to catch it. As he grabbed at the diminutive creature, the Fairy of Derry near Berry let out a piercing cry, startling Horne enough that he let go of it and it escaped into the forest. Horne also ran back home, not just without the fairy, but without a Christmas tree.

Horne apparently didn't tell anybody about the encounter, at least not anybody who would blab his story, because it didn't end up in the local paper. But six years later, in 1962, he sent the first of two letters describing the incident to Walter Webb, who worked at the Hayden Planetarium at the Boston Science Museum and was a member of various UFO groups. More than a decade later, Webb would join the team that investigated the Dover Demon in Massachusetts. Horne had heard Webb on a radio program discussing UFOs and wanted to know what Webb thought of his little green man.

Webb decided not to investigate Horne's claim, and the story ends there. One interesting coda to the story, though, is the town's name. Derry was settled by the Scotch-Irish, and it was named for a city in Ireland, a country famous for its fairy folk. So who knows? Maybe those Scotch-Irish brought over more than just their fierce distrust of government (live free or die!) and their whisky. Anyway, merry cryptid.

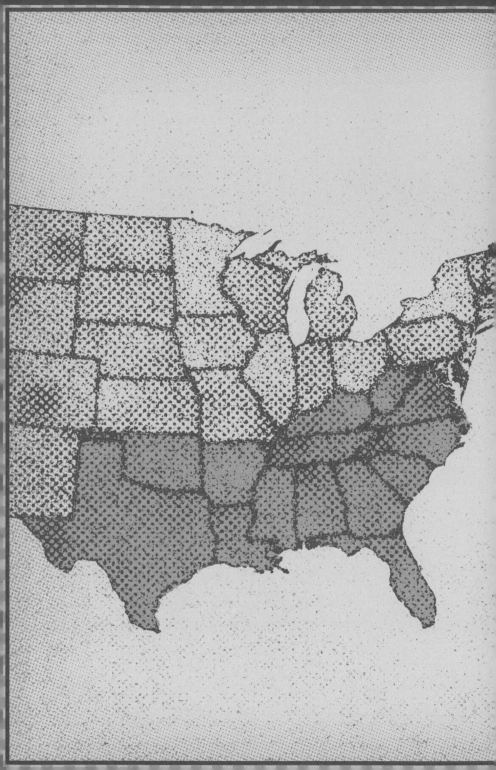

PART II.
THE SOUTH

———○———

I don't know if it's the warmer climes or diverse geography, but the wild variety of cryptids in the basement of the US is unparalleled in the country. Southern-fried cryptids trudge through the swamps and bayous, swim in the gulf and ocean, climb the mountains, and hide in the forests. The battle of the southern bigfoot is fierce, each one vying to be the most famous. The improbable Mothman rises above them all to reign as one of the most famous cryptids on the planet. In the South, you'll find insectoid, reptilian, canine, feline, humanoid, and piscine monsters, their roars and screams tinged with Cajun inflections and southern drawls and Texas twangs. Although you'll find no southern hospitality if you stumble upon one of these monsters, the Cryptid Towns of the South will certainly welcome you. Because the South is great at celebrating its cryptids.

– Fouke Monster –

THE $25 MILLION BIGFOOT

TYPE:	EARLIEST SIGHTING:
Humanoid	1971
LOCATION:	**SIZE:**
Fouke, Arkansas	6–8 feet tall

It was Saturday, the evening of May 1, 1971. Elizabeth Ford was lying on the couch at her new house, which she and her husband Bob had just moved into a week previously. It was on the outskirts of Fouke, Arkansas, isolated and surrounded by forest. The curtains on the nearby window stirred, and a long, thick, hairy arm reached through the window toward Elizabeth. She told the Associated Press, "I could see its eyes. They looked like coals of fire . . . real red." Before it had a chance to grab her, Bob and his brother Don chased what was on the other end of that arm into the woods, shotguns blasting. They had encountered what would become known as the Fouke Monster, a stinky bigfoot-type beast with long dark hair and glowing red eyes, the size of a man or bigger.

And then they encountered it again. The creature returned around midnight, ramming against the door of the house. Bob tried to fend it off, but when he went outside, the monster grabbed him. He got away and ran back to the house, so scared for his life he hit the closed front door of his home at full speed, blasting it open with his body. The incident was reported to the police and the Fords moved away the next day, the only physical evidence of the night the scratches on Bob's body. The violence and intrusive nature of the event is just one of the ways that the Fouke Monster is unique among bigfoot encounters.

Nobody else in Fouke moved away, though. They were all too busy going bigfoot crazy. Reports started to pour in of sightings of a large, dark, hairy beast haunting the farms and roads of the area and stealing livestock. Some recalled past accounts of a similar monster dating back to the 1940s. Multiple rewards were offered for its capture, including $200 by a resident named Raymond Scoggins. His condition was that the Fouke Monster had to be brought in alive so that he could put it in a zoo. T-shirts emblazoned with FOUKIE FOREVER were created by the local radio station KAAY (which also offered a $1,090 reward for its capture, the same numerals as its station number). Three men, inspired by the Ford encounter, claimed they were attacked by it, showing scratches on their bodies as evidence. A quick check of their fingernails by law enforcement belied the hoax, and they were fined. Farmers also complained to the police about damage to crops—not from the monster, but from the volume of monster hunters. Tracks were found in the area, thirteen and a half inches long and four and a half inches at their widest point. Unique not just among bigfoot but among all primate species, Foukie had only three toes on each of its big feet.

But one thing really caused the Fouke Monster to stand out amid the heyday of bigfoot sightings across the country, other than its three-toed feet and affinity for home invasion: it became a movie star. The Legend of Boggy Creek was released in 1972, just one year after the sightings. The film was the directorial debut of Charles B. Pierce, who ran an advertising agency in nearby Texarkana. He filmed the story as a docudrama, not only interviewing locals but using them as actors in reenactments. The climactic scene of the bigfoot attack was filmed in the Fords' vacated house. The movie maintains an eerie, rustic atmosphere as it shows a haunted Arkansas landscape against a trippy 1970s music soundtrack. The cheaply made ($160,000) movie eventually got a nationwide theatrical release and went on to make upward of $25 million, making the Fouke Monster famous both in cryptid circles and as a cult classic of horror film, a genre in which cryptids are just so many more monsters in a long list of them.

The movie also inspired a lot of visitors to head to Fouke to try their luck at finding the beast. Mayor J. D. Larey bemoaned to the *Hope Star* that the town of Fouke had done nothing to capitalize on the sudden monster craze. "The people here just didn't realize what they had when the iron was hot," he said. But the film did seem to cause a small resurgence in sightings. That craze would more or less dissipate by 1974, even with further Boggy Creek movies released. An unofficial 1977 sequel, *Return to Boggy Creek*, that Pierce wasn't involved in dropped the docudrama angle and starred Dawn Wells of *Gilligan's Island* fame. Pierce himself returned to film an official sequel in 1985, *Boggy Creek II: And the Legend Continues*.

Meanwhile, the people of Fouke learned their lesson about capitalizing on their local monster. If you visit Fouke today, you can head to the Fouke Monster Mart, a museum and store dedicated to the beast and other related cryptids. And if you come at the right time in the summer, you can attend the Fouke Monster Festival, where they party in honor of their local legend with concerts, talks by cryptozoologists, guided tours, and, of course, screenings of *The Legend of Boggy Creek*.

– Wampus Cat –

WE'VE GOT CRYPTIDS, YES WE DO!

TYPE:	EARLIEST SIGHTING:
Feline	Prehistory
LOCATION:	**NOTABLE FEATURE:**
Arkansas	Four- or six-legged

Big cats are an entire category of cryptid. They're also called alien big cats (ABCs) and refer to scientifically verified big cats—cheetahs, tigers, jaguars—that are either thought to be extinct or are witnessed in regions where they shouldn't exist—like panthers in New England, for instance, despite going extinct there a hundred years ago. Or American lions in the Midwest, even though they've been nothing but fossils for at least 10,000 years. And then there's the wampus cat, a big cat that shouldn't be anywhere, but is apparently everywhere.

Wampus cat has become a catch-all term for any large, strange cat. Sometimes it's an ABC or sometimes an ordinary big cat that wasn't seen clearly enough to identify it. However, its physical form, when described, is just as slippery. Sometimes it's bipedal. Sometimes it has a ball at the end of its tail. Sometimes it has six legs. It's always fierce—a creature to be avoided like any big cat—and it's been seen mostly in the South, although legends and reports have also placed it, well, just about everywhere else. I'm letting Arkansas claim it for a specific reason that we'll get to in a moment.

The bipedal version of the wampus cat is often connected to various stories attributed to the Cherokee, all involving the transformation of a woman. In one tale, a woman spies on a sacred male hunting ritual and is punished by being fused with the mountain lion hide she is wearing. In another, a witch who turns herself into a cat to commit crimes is interrupted midchange and stays a cat-woman forever. In a third, a superhero-like origin story, a woman wears a cat mask to protect her husband from a witch and eventually melds with the mask to become a cat-woman who guards against evil.

But there is an even stranger feature of the wampus cat. Stranger than subsuming all other strange cat encounters, stranger than being used in folklore to depict female punishment or empowerment, and that is: the wampus cat has become a favorite mascot for high schools across the nation. Leesville High School in Leesville, Louisiana, is one of them, depicting it as a fierce yellow bobcat. Itasca High School in Itasca, Texas, is another. The Texan wampus cat is also yellow, but shaped like a tiger. A statue on the grounds of the school shows it standing on two legs, either in a nod to the bipedal form of the wampus cat or just as typical mascot anthropomorphism. Atoka High School in Atoka, Oklahoma, sports another bobcat-like creature in the school colors of either yellow or burgundy. But the wampus cat mascot doesn't get truly weird until we arrive at Clark Fork High School in Clark Fork, Idaho. Its wampus cat is a yellow cougar with a spiked mace on the end of its tail. A large mural in the gymnasium shows off the creature in all its dangerous glory.

But of all those high schools, only one has learned the lesson that so many Cryptid Towns have learned: it's the statue of your monster that really counts. Conway High School in

Conway, Arkansas, chose a form of wampus cat that would give it a leg up on other wampus cats. Two legs up, actually. Their six-legged panther is a vicious beast. The school has long displayed a rough-hewn metal sculpture in the sky-blue of the school colors on the grounds of its sports field. But in January 2013, they went (six) steps further and erected a realistic six-foot-tall bronze statue of the six-legged cat that would make any Cryptid Town jealous.

Created by artist Raymond Gibby, the cat sits on a pedestal in the center of a roundabout in the middle of campus. A plaque on the pedestal reads:

> WAMPUS CAT
> *A mythical,*
> *cat-like creature*
> *with six legs:*
> *four for running*
> *at the speed of light,*
> *two for fighting*
> *with all its might.*

Go Wampus Cats!

– Mothman –

HARBINGER OF HORROR

TYPE:	EARLIEST SIGHTING:
Aerial-humanoid	1966
LOCATION:	SIZE:
Point Pleasant, West Virginia	6–7 feet tall

It was a hot and buggy August night in Point Pleasant, West Virginia. I was standing under a giant cement dome in the middle of a forest, my only light a weak electric lantern. The bunker had once held wartime explosives, possibly industrial waste as well. Now it was an empty, abandoned cavern covered in graffitied warnings about a monster. I was deep in the lair of the Mothman.

The Mothman is one of the most famous cryptids in the country. It's the punk rock to Bigfoot's disco. The story of the Mothman begins like many classic cryptid stories, with teens in a car on a back road at night. The night was November 15, 1966. The back road was in the TNT area of Point Pleasant, West Virginia, so called because of the immense concrete igloos that dot the forest, which had been used to store munitions during World War II and later chemical waste from factories. The teens were Roger and Linda Scarberry and Steve and Mary Mallette, two young married couples cruising the dirt roads looking for some action. Instead, they found the Mothman.

They saw its eyes first—two glowing red circles in the dark. And then they saw the rest of it: six or seven feet tall, gray, two muscular humanlike legs, bat wings folded against its back. It was standing outside the gates of an old, abandoned power plant. They sped off, their 1957 Chevy spitting dirt, but passed the creature again on a small hill. The monster rose straight into the air without a single beat of its large wings and pursued them, wings still motionless, more like a ghost than a giant moth. Making eerie, high-pitched squeaking sounds, the creature kept up with the car, despite them hitting 100 miles per hour once they reached the straight asphalt of Route 62. The Mothman followed them all the way to town before disappearing into the dark. The four teenagers stumbled into the sheriff's office, spilling their tale, so terrified they didn't care how crazy it sounded.

The police held a press conference the next day. The news went national. A newspaper editor dubbed the creature "Mothman" and the name caught on—the whole country had Batman on the brain thanks to the *Batman* television series starring Adam West and Burt Ward that had debuted earlier that year. Locals and tourists and news crews crowded the TNT area, looking for the creature—and many found it.

It chased a family by the name of Wamsley into a friend's house a mile from the TNT area. A group of teenagers saw it perched on the edge of a quarry. A shoe salesman named Thomas Ury drove by it on Route 62 and watched it fly straight up into the night sky, circle his car, and dive at him, chasing him for miles. Another man saw it on his front lawn and staggered back inside, pale and scared and close to a heart attack. The stories go on and on. The sighting by the Scarberrys and the Mallettes kicked off thirteen months of high-density strangeness in the Point Pleasant area and more than one hundred witnesses of the gray ghost.

The people of Point Pleasant weren't just being dive-bombed by a demon in the dark, they were witnessing men in black, UFOs, ghosts, livestock mutilations, and more. It was like all the weirdness in the world had descended on Mason County for a convention of the strange, with Mothman as guest of honor. That weirdness was chronicled by journalist John Keel, who traveled to Point Pleasant from his home in Manhattan after reading about the sightings. He would go on to write *The Mothman Prophecies*, a nonfiction account of the odd occurrences of that year. It hit the *New York Times* best-seller list and was adapted into a 2002 film starring Richard Gere.

Plenty of theories were offered for who or what the Mothman was: a new species, an extraterrestrial, a sandhill crane, a barn owl, a mutant survivor of power plant runoff or the sludge stored in the TNT bunkers, an extradimensional traveler. And eventually, a harbinger of horror. On December 15, 1967, the Silver Bridge collapsed. The mile-long span connecting Point Pleasant with Gallipolis, Ohio, across the Ohio River was fully laden with Christmas shoppers and commuters. Forty-six people died at the bottom of that icy river. The ensuing inquest discovered a tiny flaw in one of the eyebars of the thirty-nine-year-old bridge.

After the tragedy, reports of the Mothman petered out, causing some to hypothesize that the creature was sent to warn locals of the impending disaster. Or perhaps the people of Point Pleasant and Gallipolis simply had bigger concerns than Mothman in the wake of that tragic loss of life. But somehow the tragedy gave the story of the Mothman something that few cryptid tales ever get: a climax.

Well, sort of. Sporadic sightings of the Mothman continue to this day, not only in West Virginia but in other states, including Illinois and Minnesota. However, the people of Point Pleasant have made sure that the majority of Mothman sightings stay firmly in West Virginia. In the middle of town is a gleaming twelve-foot-tall, stainless steel statue with an insectoid head and large red eyes, a bipedal body bursting with superhero muscles and well-formed buttocks, and tall wings like rotted sails. Adjacent to the statue is the Mothman Museum, which is full of newspaper clippings, props from the Richard Gere movie, and artifacts from John Keel's collection. Throughout town are memorials to the Silver Bridge Disaster, including bronze plaques and a mural, while its replacement—the Silver Memorial Bridge—looms in the distance.

Beyond these fixtures, every September since 2002, Point Pleasant has thrown its Mothman Festival. Ten thousand people descend on this town of 4,000 to party, cosplay, shop, and attend tours and lectures. It's the most successful cryptid festival in the country and has inspired many other towns to organize festivals feting their fearsome fiends.

Back in the TNT area, I saw plenty of moths, but no Mothman. I was accompanied on my mission by my eleven-year-old daughter, Esme, who was wearing the Mothman T-shirt she had bought at the museum gift shop that afternoon. After we left the creepily echoing bunkers, we saw flashlight beams in the distance. Probably more tourists, drawn to the town and its monster like so many moths to the flame.

Is Mothman a Ghost?

If you want to frustrate a cryptozoologist, ask them the same question that police ask murder suspects: "Where's the body?" A cryptid corpse is the one piece of evidence needed to conclusively prove any cryptid hypothesis. And while most cryptozoologists keep looking, other cryptid aficionados get creative. Or maybe desperate. Or perhaps mischievous. They posit other theories about cryptids to get around the body problem.

What if cryptids are ghosts? Ghosts don't leave corpses (you know what I mean). That would explain why bigfoot continue to evade capture, and why Mothman and batsquatch and giant sky clams can take flight against all laws of physics.

What if cryptids are aliens? It's myopic and possibly prejudiced to believe that every creature from the stars is short, bulbous-headed, and big-eyed. Maybe they look like the Van Meter Visitor. Or the Enfield Monster. Why this panoply of alien beings is on Earth is anyone's guess. Maybe they just needed to take their hodag out for a walk after that cramped flying saucer ride across the galaxy.

What if cryptids are extradimensional entities? Creatures or beings that step sideways into this dimension, and then step sideways out of it? Sometimes these creatures are called ultraterrestrials. John Keel, the chronicler of Mothman and all the weirdness surrounding its Point Pleasant appearance, was a proponent of this theory. His 1975 book *The Eighth Tower: On Ultraterrestrials and the Superspectrum* attempted to provide a unifying theory behind everything from UFOs to ghosts to demons to cryptids.

In the thought exercise that is Occam's razor, if you have multiple theories, the one with the fewest assumptions is probably correct. With these theories, it's the opposite: when your weird explanation doesn't pan out, go weirder.

–Flatwoods Monster –

"FRANKENSTEIN WITH B.O."

TYPE:	EARLIEST SIGHTING:
Alien	1952
LOCATION:	**SIZE:**
Flatwoods, West Virginia	10 feet tall

My first clue that I was in a Cryptid Town was the gas station. Inside the shop, an entire shelf was filled with eight-inch-tall red and green ceramic lanterns. They looked like Christmas tree toppers at first, but they weren't. They were flame-headed monsters in green dresses. The Flatwoods Monster is a weird creature, even in a book about weird creatures. That's because it's a cryptid, or an alien, or possibly a robot—in a dress. So an alien cryptid robot in a dress. I just had to invite that thing to this party.

The Flatwoods Monster earned its invitation on the evening of September 12, 1952, in the tiny town of Flatwoods, West Virginia. Five boys ranging in age from ten to fourteen were playing outside the elementary school near dark when they saw what every child playing outside wants to see: a UFO. The fiery object streaked across the sky and seemed to land on a hill at a neighboring farm. They rushed to the spot, picking up Kathleen May (the mother of two of the boys) on the way, as well as a seventeen-year-old West Virginia National Guardsman named Gene Lemon. The intrepid seven, along with a dog named Richie, took off into the dark forest on humankind's first intergalactic diplomacy mission.

At the top of the hill they could see a glowing object, and upon arrival the group found themselves surrounded by an odd mist that was tinged by a strobing red light, giving the hilltop an eerie, dreamlike quality. An awful metallic smell pervaded the area. Something by a nearby tree caught Lemon's attention, so he shined his flashlight at it—to reveal our alien robot cryptid in a dress. It was ten feet tall with long thin claws and round, glowing eyes set into a round red face cowled in a spade-shaped hood. Its body was covered in a green, metallic material that ended in a pleated skirt. Later Kathleen May would describe it this way: "It looked worse than Frankenstein. It couldn't have been human." The description prompted the *Statesville Daily Record* to dub the creature a "Frankenstein monster with B.O." due to the stench on the hill. Later, the party maintained that based on the metallic sheen and the way it moved, it was undoubtedly a robot. And it definitely moved—the Flatwoods Monster hissed and floated toward the terrified group. First contact was over. The group fled back to the May residence, where they found themselves sick for days after with nausea and other symptoms.

The hill was soon covered with local police, the National Guard, ufologists, and various townsfolk, all investigating this strange incident. The only evidence found of the encounter was trampled grass, a set of skid marks, and an oil-like residue. There is some disagreement over whether the odor was still present when investigators arrived. Newspapers across the country ran the story, and Kathleen May and Gene Lemon were flown to Manhattan to appear on a TV show, which featured an artist's conception of the Flatwoods Monster that would become iconic.

Seventy years later, the Flatwoods Monster completely infests the town—and not just at the gas stations. Flatwoods welcomes visitors with a sign that says HOME OF THE GREEN MONSTER, which is another name for the Flatwoods Monster, as are the Braxton County Monster and the Phantom of Flatwoods. In town you'll find a restaurant and ice cream shop called The Spot. Its menu has an entire section of UFO-themed sandwiches. Outside, a massive plywood billboard is emblazoned with the Flatwoods Monster and two people with their faces cut out so that visitors can stick their heads in the holes for a photo op.

But the most important stop in the Flatwoods Monster tour is not in Flatwoods. It's next door in Sutton. As you drive through, you'll see large throne-like wooden chairs along the road painted to look like the monster. You can take a break from all your monster hunting to sit on its lap, but not for too long: you have to get to Main Street, which is the site of the Flatwoods Monster Museum. It features ephemera and artifacts from the encounter, life-sized recreations of the monster, and souvenirs for purchase—including, of course, those ceramic lanterns.

Every year Sutton throws a Flatwoods Monster Fest. Well, not every year. In 2020, when every festival on the planet—cryptid or otherwise—was canceled during the COVID-19 pandemic, the Flatwoods Monster still managed to make an appearance, saving a glass-blowing shop in Milton, West Virginia, from bankruptcy. The Blenko Glass Company was on the verge of becoming another COVID-19 victim when it decided to do a limited run of 800 glass Flatwood Monsters. The 16.5-inch green and red cryptids sold out fast, and Blenko's COVID year turned out to be its most profitable one in decades. And while I missed out on the Blenko piece, I did get myself a Flatwoods Monster lantern. It looks great atop my Christmas tree.

‒Skunk Ape‒

BIGFOOT'S EMBARRASSING COUSIN

TYPE:	EARLIEST SIGHTING:
Humanoid	1920s
LOCATION:	**SIZE:**
Everglades, Florida	7–8 feet tall, 350–700 pounds

The skunk ape of the Florida Everglades doesn't get its name from a cool pair of white racing stripes down its furry back. It comes in all the usual drab shades of bigfoot-esque monsters—brown, red, and dark. The skunk ape's name comes, unfortunately, from its smell. All the worst smells have been used to describe its stench: wet dog, rotten eggs, excrement, even decaying corpses. Maybe the smell is inherent and serves a biological purpose, or maybe it has something to do with Florida's baking heat and the fetidness of the sticky swamplands that the creature calls home. Meanwhile, its bigfoot cousins in the Pacific Northwest tromp through pine-scented forests refreshed by annual snowfalls.

But that doesn't mean the skunk ape is any less lovable than the bigfoot—and nobody seems to love it more than Dave Shealy. The native Floridian rose to prominence in the cryptid community in 1998 when he took twenty-seven photos of a dark form in the swamp while on a months-long stakeout for the creature. In 2000, he also released a video of a dark humanoid form loping through the swamp. He claims his sightings of the creature date back to 1974 when he was ten years old. He and his older brother Jack were tramping through the swamp and saw a dark creature about a hundred yards away. Jack had to lift the younger Shealy over the tall swamp grass so that he could see. It wasn't a long look, though, as a rainstorm began almost immediately, driving the monster back into the thicker swamp.

The Shealy brothers were so inspired by the skunk ape that in 1994 they opened the Skunk Ape Research Headquarters, a swampside attraction in the town of Ochopee on the edge of the Big Cypress National Preserve. At the Skunk Ape Research Headquarters, you'll find all the usual cryptid displays and accessories: footprint casts, statues, blurry photos, newspaper reports, toys, T-shirts, and mugs. But the center also boasts a distinctive Florida flair, including preserved alligator heads, live reptiles, and swamp tours. It's even got a camping ground, so you can learn about the creature and then wait for it in the night. You'll know it by the smell.

And while the late 1990s were a good time for skunk ape watchers (a group of half a dozen tourists saw one in 1997 while on a van tour of the Everglades), the skunk ape existed in folklore long before the Shealy brothers. Some trace it all the way back to Seminole and Miccosukee lore or the stories of Everglades fishers and trappers in the early 1920s, but the skunk ape as we smell him—seven to eight feet tall, bipedal, 350 to 450 pounds—really rose to prominence in the 1970s, like most of its counterparts across the country. Some credit this timing to a nationwide bigfoot mania (sparked by the release of the iconic 1967 Patterson-Gimlin footage of a bigfoot in Bluff Creek, California—see page 222), and others to the fact that intensive development of the Everglades began in that decade.

The first sighting that really put the skunk ape in the papers was in February 1971, three years before the Shealy brothers' initial sighting. An electronics engineer and amateur archeologist by the name of H. C. Osborn was out in the swamp with four others, digging for relics in a Native American mound in the same Big Cypress Swamp where the Skunk Ape Research Headquarters is today. At three in the morning, the group heard noises outside their tents. They exited to find a seven-foot-tall, seven-hundred-pound skunk ape standing there and staring at them. Before anybody could react, the creature darted off into the dark swamp. The next morning, the crew made plaster casts of nearby footprints and determined that there had to be least three skunk apes in the area.

Besides its odor and its name, other elements of the skunk ape story diverge from more traditional hairy hominids. Sometimes knuckle prints are found pressed into the soft mud, complete with opposable thumbs. Some say the creature is arboreal, and that's how it traverses such a treacherous landscape. But the skunk ape has one other thing going for it: you'd have to be an extremely dedicated hoaxer to put on a stifling, smelly gorilla suit in the middle of a swamp in the burning Florida heat.

«———◆———»

– Lizard Man –

THE SCALY SCOURGE OF
SCAPE ORE SWAMP

TYPE:	**EARLIEST SIGHTING:**
Reptilian-humanoid	1988
LOCATION:	**SIZE:**
Bishopville, South Carolina	7 feet tall

The Lizard Man of Scape Ore Swamp is a seven-foot-tall, scaly green humanoid with glowing red eyes who likes to claw up cars in South Carolina. Or perhaps it's just a bespectacled man wrapped in a burlap blanket trying to stop thieves from taking his air conditioners (we'll get to that in a bit). You decide.

Scape Ore Swamp is 100 square miles of wetland just north of Sumter. Throughout the 1980s, rumors of a scaly monster roaming the swamp were passed around the tiny town of Bishopville, which sits right on the edge of Scape Ore. But it wasn't until July 1988 that things got really reptilian. Tom and Mary Waye, who lived near Scape Ore, woke up to discover that the 1985 Ford LTD in their carport had been scratched and dented, wires ripped from the engine and molding torn off. It looked more like it had been chewed by an animal than vandalized by a person. Locals placed their bets on various creatures that could have inflicted the damage, from foxes to bears, but someone from the crowd of people who had gathered to watch the investigation offered, "What about the Lizard Man?"

Intrigued, Sheriff Liston Truesdale of the Lee County Sheriff's office was more interested in investigating this monster than foxes and bears. He sent out a call for information and was immediately rewarded with a list of people who had witnessed the Lizard Man over the years. He didn't need the list for long, because two days later, seventeen-year-old Christopher Davis came by the station. The story Davis told the sheriff not only gave form to the monster that haunted Scape Ore Swamp, but turned it into an international sensation.

A month earlier, Davis was driving home at 2:30 a.m. from the late shift at McDonald's, a bag full of Filet-O-Fish sandwiches in the passenger seat. After crossing Scape Ore Swamp bridge on Browntown Road, the car started wobbling, and Davis pulled over. He got out of the car and confirmed his fear: flat tire.

He set to work, swapping out the limp rubber for the spare in the muggy, dark South Carolina night. He was throwing everything in the trunk after finishing the repair when he saw something sinister across a butter bean field—and then it ran at him. According to the *Afro-American*, a local newspaper in the Carolinas, Davis described the creature as "green, wet-like, about seven feet tall . . . three fingers, red eyes, skin like a lizard and snakelike scales." Terrified, he hopped into the car, only to see the monster at the window. It jumped atop the car, its three-fingered claws scrabbling down the windshield. Davis smashed the accelerator, knocking the thing off his car. He estimated he was going about thirty-five miles an hour, but the creature kept pace, again jumping atop the car. Swerving and speeding up, Davis was finally able to throw the monster back into the swamp. He sped home, where he immediately told his parents about his close encounter of the cryptid kind.

After he told the sheriff, Davis's story got out—and out—and out, and soon major media outlets across the world were stoking Lizard Man fever. They descended on the tiny town, attracting mobs of tourists as they came. Businesses started selling Lizard Man merchandise. Davis himself got a manager and did paid appearances. A radio station offered a million-dollar reward for the creature, causing hunters from all over the country to eschew their usual game for whatever lurked in Scape Ore Swamp.

Meanwhile, more cars were damaged overnight by mysterious claws, and more witnesses came forward. Lots of people reported seeing a large form crossing the roads of Scape Ore. Interestingly, other than Davis's account, the reptilian aspect of the creature wasn't usually reported by witnesses, causing some cryptozoologists to wonder if the creature wasn't just another run-of-the-mill bigfoot. But Davis's scaly description elevated the occurrence to something new, something more interesting—something more terrifying.

Amidst all the Lizard Man excitement, some locals doubted the story immediately—because they might have heard from the Lizard Man itself. Davis blew his tire near a butter bean farm owned by a man named Lucious Elmore. Elmore claimed he had chased a thief out of his field the very night that Davis had his encounter. Apparently, Elmore had recently equipped the shed where he dried his butter beans with new air conditioners, items which were expensive and extremely vulnerable to theft, especially in the swampy South Carolina summer. To protect the equipment, Elmore slept in the shed, wrapped in a burlap blanket. When he heard a car pull off to the side of the road not one hundred yards from his shed, the six-foot-plus man went out to chase away any would-be thieves, wrapped in his burlap blanket, eyeglasses flashing. The thief spotted him in the field and immediately screamed and took off in his car, possibly scratching it up on low hanging branches or leaving the jack attached to the car in his haste to get away. Maybe that's the other side of the story. Maybe not.

Regardless, a man guarding his AC units held nothing over the narrative power of a humanoid reptile jacking up cars in the night. But even that narrative could only hold for so long. By the early 1990s, Lizard Man sightings had died down, although anytime a car gets chewed up near the swamp, as it has here and there over the years, the people of Bishopville are forced to wonder if the creature is back.

These days, the town of Bishopville throws a Lizard Man Festival, hoping to coax the cryptid out of hiding (or visitors into buying). But even if you can't time your visit to enjoy the festival, you can easily theme your day in Bishopville around the Lizard Man. Start off with lunch at Harry and Harry Two, a restaurant featuring menu items inspired by the beast (its tagline: FEED YOUR INNER LIZARDMAN). Outside the restaurant, a wrought-iron sign depicts the Lizard Man boiling something in a cauldron. Then, you can hit up the South Carolina Cotton Museum. They have a larger-than-life boll weevil statue that would be the weirdest thing there, if it weren't for the Lizard Man. The museum features a small exhibit including three-toed footprint casts, T-shirts, and an Elmore Butter Bean sign.

Then, of course, you can swing by Scape Ore Swamp itself, especially the bridge area. Just check your tires first and don't be carrying any Filet-O-Fish sandwiches—just in case the monster has a taste for them.

— Altamaha-ha —

WATER MONSTER MASH-UP

TYPE:	EARLIEST SIGHTING:
Aquatic	1830
LOCATION:	**SIZE:**
Darien, Georgia	20–30 feet long

Georgia has 110 miles of glowing ocean coast. However, despite all that beachfront access, its most famous aquatic monster took up residence in one of its rivers—and one of its visitor centers.

The tiny city of Darien (population: 1,975) is located at the delta where the state's largest river, the Altamaha (named for a Yamasee chief) terminates at the Atlantic Ocean after flowing 137 miles from the confluence of the Oconee and Ocmulgee Rivers. There, at the midpoint of the Georgia coast, the "Amazon of the South" forms a swampy area of islands and canals and ponds and marshes—the perfect hiding place for a monster.

Over the centuries, a large, serpentine creature has been spotted in those labyrinthine waterways. Its name is Altamaha-ha, or Altie. Like most cryptid tales, the story is supposed to originate with the indigenous peoples, but, interestingly enough, Darien was settled by Scottish highlanders out of Inverness, a city at the mouth of Loch Ness. In fact, the original name of Darien was New Inverness. Maybe one of those highlanders brought over some Nessie tadpoles with them.

Regardless, in the written record, sightings began in the mid-nineteenth century with a Captain Delano. In 1830, Delano, who captained a schooner called the *Eagle*, told the *Georgian* newspaper of Savannah that he had witnessed a large monster about seventy feet long at St. Simons Island, right at the mouth of the Altamaha River. He described it as the width of a sugar barrel, with an alligator-like head. The sighting was backed up by both members of his crew and farmers on the island. When it was suggested that he might have just seen one of the whales which frequent the area, the old salt got salty and explained that he was a sea captain and knew what a whale looked like. I assume he ended the response with, "ye scabby sea bass."

A hundred years later, sightings started up again with some regularity as more people explored the delta and used it for logging, hunting, and fishing. Over time, witness reports described a monster that looked more like a plesiosaur than a sea serpent, which was the case with many aquatic monsters after the discovery of dinosaurs. Witnesses gave it a bony ridge atop its back, the snout of a crocodile, and long sharp teeth. Its size has been clocked anywhere from fifteen feet to Captain Delano's seventy feet, although the general consensus is twenty to thirty feet. The most interesting element of its anatomy, though, is that it has only two limbs, a pair of flippers up front and nothing but a sinuous tail in the back, making it sort of a wet centaur—plesiosaur up front, sea serpent in the back, and far more distinct (and ownable) than other water monsters across the country as a result.

In December 1980, a former newspaper editor named Larry Gwin claimed to have seen Altie while fishing for eels in the river with a friend. He described it as fifteen to twenty feet long, the circumference of a person, and with two brown humps on its back. However, a 1981 article in the *Atlantic Constitution* offers that, according to Gwin, it wasn't seen in the river but instead in his own newspaper-editor imagination as he hung out at a local restaurant fishing for rubes.

In May 1998, three eleven-year-old boys witnessed perhaps the closest sighting of Altie on record. Rusty Davis, Bennett Bacon, and Owen Lynch were preparing to jump into the river for a swim when they saw a gray-brown monster covered in slimy vegetation emerge from the river. Well, Davis and Lynch saw it—Bacon had already dived in. His friends shouted at him in a panic, and Bacon turned to see a large sinewy tail not ten feet away. Bacon immediately reversed course and sprang back onto dry land. All three children survived to tell their tale to a Saturday afternoon television show called *Real Scary Stories*.

But you don't have to dip your toes in the delta to see the creature with your own eyes. A billboard in Darien sports an image of the two-flippered creature and directs travelers to the Darien-McIntosh Regional Visitor Information Center. There, dominating a space mostly used for tourist attraction pamphlets and public restrooms, is a twenty-foot-long fiberglass statue of the monster, dramatically posed and ready for photo ops.

The model was created by Rick Spears in 2009, but he wasn't the only artist to get in on the Altie game. In 2018, an eviscerated baby Altie-shaped corpse was found on the shore of Wolf Island, near Darien. After people puzzled over the photos for days, it was revealed to be an installation by performance artist Zardulu. The piece was called *Ketos Troias* after a sea monster in Greek myth that Heracles slices open with a fishhook. Zardulu told Vice.com that she wanted to "breathe some new life into the legend." Based on the record, though, belief in Altie has plenty of life.

– Moon-Eyed People –

ANCIENT ALABASTER ALIENS

TYPE:	EARLIEST SIGHTING:
Humanoid	Prehistory
LOCATION:	**NOTABLE FEATURE:**
Fort Mountain, Georgia; Murphy, North Carolina	Sensitivity to sunlight

Who were the Moon-Eyed People? Aliens from space? A prehistoric race? Cherokee myths? Cryptid-beings? Were they Welsh?

The Moon-Eyed People pop up here and there in European settler accounts from the eighteenth century, always based on secondhand Cherokee stories, though, and not firsthand experience. The idea became more widespread in 1902 when James Mooney, an ethnographer who studied Native American culture extensively and lived with the Cherokee in North Carolina for many years, published a work called Myths of the Cherokee.

One of the myths that Mooney recorded was the story of the Moon-Eyed People. It was a short account, about four hundred words. In it, Mooney relays that when the Cherokee arrived in what is now the southeast area of the United States, they found another people living there. That race was short, pale, possibly albino. And they only came out at night, because their eyes couldn't take sunlight—hence the name.

The Moon-Eyed People seemed to be nice enough

neighbors. They built circular houses out of logs covered in dirt, as well as some forts. They also warned the Cherokee of a giant leech-like creature that lived in the river. But for some reason (not included in Mooney's tale), the Cherokee didn't get along with them. Maybe they found their pale skin and big eyes creepy. Maybe they just wanted all the land to themselves. Eventually the Moon-Eyed People were chased off by the Cherokee, never to be seen again, by the light of the moon or the sun.

But there is another legend from another time and another people that crashes its car into this one. It starts across the Atlantic Ocean. In Welsh lore first documented in 1559 in the *Cronica Walliae*—a history of Wales aggregated by Humphrey Llwyd—a prince named Madog ap Llewellyn settled the Americas in 1170, centuries before Columbus tripped over the tiny island of Guanahaní. Madog explored what is now southern Appalachia, built houses there, and established a settlement. Of course, being Welsh, the people were pale, especially in the eyes of the Cherokee who had not encountered Europeans before.

So the story goes that the Moon-Eyed People were just Welsh settlers—although the Welsh usually can see okay in the daylight. In this version of the story, they weren't chased away by the Cherokee. They just eventually interbred the pale skin out of the population, so that when the rest of Europe arrived half a millennium later, there were no other whiteys, moon-eyed or otherwise. British leaders used the legend as proof of the legitimacy of their claim on the New World, and Thomas Jefferson explicitly asked Lewis and Clark in a letter to keep an eye out for "Welsh Indians."

However it started, the lore of the Moon-Eyed People lives on in the mountains of Appalachia to this day. At Fort Mountain in north Georgia, for instance, are the mysterious ruins of stone structures. Some say the Moon-Eyed People built them. Historical placards in the area tell the story of the Moon-Eyed People, pretty much as Mooney told it, although in this variation the Moon-Eyed People can see fine during the day, but go blind during certain phases of the moon. It was during one of those phases that the Cherokee killed them all.

In 1840, sixty miles northwest and across the state border in the town of Murphy, North Carolina, a mysterious statue was unearthed during a land-clearing project. The soapstone statue of unknown origin and age depicts two standing beings cojoined at the hip, each about three feet tall with oversized round heads and large eyes. Some say it's a depiction of two Moon-Eyed People (other theories say space aliens or fairy folk). If it is an accurate representation, the Moon-Eyed People were also a Moon-Headed People. The statue was held in private hands until 2015, when it joined the collection of the Cherokee Valley Historical Museum in Murphy, where it can be seen today—perhaps the only surviving testament to the ancient nocturnal cryptid-beings.

– Beast of Bladenboro –

DRACULA'S CAT

TYPE:	EARLIEST SIGHTING:
Feline	1954
LOCATION:	**SIZE:**
Bladenboro, North Carolina	3–5 feet long, 90–150 pounds

Some cryptids appear briefly, spook a few townsfolk, and then melt quietly back into the night. Other cryptids, like the Beast of Bladenboro, crash onto the scene with astonishing violence.

In January 1954 in the town of Bladenboro, North Carolina, three dogs were discovered with their skulls crushed flat and tongues chewed out. But it wasn't until somebody cut open the poor canines that they discovered something even more disturbing. According to the *Robesonian* newspaper, Police Chief Roy Fores explained that the dogs had been almost completely exsanguinated. The same word popped into everybody's head at this revelation, but Fores was the first to use it on record: vampire. He immediately tried to drain the terror from the word, though, adding: "The vampire is probably a mad wolf."

Posses were formed to support Fores as he searched the swamplands on the edge of town for what the newspapers variously called a "vampire beast" or "vampire killer" or the "bleeder beast of Bladenboro." None of those hunting parties could find the creature. Somehow, though, many of the dogs in town did.

Over the course of the next month, up to a dozen dogs were killed, some decapitated, some drained of blood, and others mauled. Footprints in the snow included long, heavy claw marks, and people started seeing a dark-coated, cat-faced creature between three and five feet long and between 90 and 150 pounds, the size of a large dog. The beast's cry sounded like that of a baby or a woman in distress, but of a timbre that communicated in no uncertain terms that its source was not human.

About a thousand hunters came from miles around to bag the beast, outnumbering the local residents by a good couple hundred. The hunters even brought dogs as bait. For one dog, it worked too well, as it was dragged off into the swamp by the creature within earshot of a hunting party that was powerless to stop it. Newspapers reported that Bladenboro had turned into a carnival, although probably not the kind of carnival you want to bring your kids to.

Many hypothesized about the types of large cats that the beast could be—panther, lynx, bobcat, catamount, mountain lion—but none of these animals quite fit the profile. Those types of cats were either extremely rare in Bladenboro or weren't so violently confrontational. One veterinarian posited that it might not be a cat at all, but an escaped watchdog on a bloodlust-fueled killing spree.

Some found humor in the situation. The *News and Observer* quotes an unnamed man as saying, "Before the beast came, my wife and I had twin beds." And the local theater owner (who was also the mayor) made sure not only to run *The Big Cat*, a 1949 action movie about a puma, but to take out a newspaper ad about it that read:

NOW YOU CAN SEE THE 'CAT'!

Its first attack on a human was on January 5 at eight p.m. Mrs. C. E. Kinlaw was outside her house investigating some whimpering dogs. She saw the creature, which she described as a "big mountain lion." It charged at her. She screamed. It stalled in its tracks, and, as her husband dashed outside, it ran off. They examined its tracks later and learned something newly disturbing: there were two sets. The *Asheville Citizen-Times* paper summarized the discovery succinctly as: "the vampire may have a mate." There were two Beasts of Bladenboro out there.

Eventually, all those hunters in town became annoying and dangerous, so Officer Flores called off the grand hunt. Newspapers announced it with the headline, VAMPIRE BEAST WINS BATTLE OF BLADENBORO. Not long after, a thirty-five-pound bobcat was killed, as was a similarly sized "leopard-like" animal that some claimed was an ocelot. People touted one or both of those animals as the Beast. When pigs and chickens were violently killed in the ensuing days, others took that as proof that the Beast was still out there. By the end of January, there were no more sightings of the beast, although for the rest of the year, any time livestock were killed, people wondered if it had returned.

So was it a bobcat or ocelot after all? Maybe. But one thing is for sure: Bladenboro doesn't celebrate a Bobcat Fest every year. It celebrates a Beast Fest. In 2009, Bladenboro kicked off an annual celebration of the mysterious animal. Every fall, 8,000 people converge on this town of less than 2,000 to listen to music, eat food, wear costumes, participate in carnival activities, and get a picture with the festival mascot, a person costumed as the Beast of Bladenboro, which they affectionately call B.O.B.

– Norfolk Mermaid –

FABRICATED FISHFOLK

TYPE:	CREATED:
Sculptural	1999
LOCATION:	**MATERIAL:**
Norfolk, Virginia	Fiberglass

The city of Norfolk, Virginia, has embraced the mermaid as its mascot, although no one in the city has ever seen one. The archetype of the mermaid spans the globe and dates back thousands of years. It is most often imagined as half woman, half fish (top and bottom, respectively), although there are various permutations on the form and gender. The mermaid is often considered more of a fantasy creature than a true cryptid, although cryptozoologists have posited various cryptids as the source of the mermaid myth—everything from undiscovered species of pale seals to aquatic primates.

Norfolk is one of the few big cities in this book. At a quarter of a million residents, it's the third largest city in the state and hovers around the eightieth largest in the country. It occupies seven miles of the mouth of the Chesapeake, and the country's biggest naval base is there—Naval Station Norfolk. If mermaids ever attacked from the water, the city would be ready.

But Norfolk's embrace of the mermaid wasn't the result of some terrifying night in the 1970s when fish-beings slopped up on the Chesapeake shores. No teenagers drove their boats across obscure waterways late at night and saw fins and glowing red eyes. No colonial-era mischaracterization of the fauna of the New World resulted in mermaid mania. It was purely a business decision.

On November 30, 1999, at a lunch event of 300 local business and government leaders, an attorney named Peter Decker (known locally as Uncle Pete) proposed an idea that his wife Bess had suggested to him after visiting Chicago. In the Windy City, Bess had witnessed the newly installed "Cows on Parade" public art exhibit, a series of 300 fiberglass cows dotting the city. They had been manufactured by the city and sold to local businesses, who then hired artists to decorate them. The goal of the exhibit was to encourage residents and tourists to visit all the cows, as well as the businesses and organizations that sponsored them. The event raised millions of dollars for charity and served as a unifying element for the city. The now-named Cow-Parade has since gone global and been adapted by hundreds of cities.

At that Norfolk breakfast, though, they zagged away from the cow aspect and zigged toward the fantastical. "Why don't we become Mermaid City?" they proposed. The Deckers liked the idea because mermaids were nautical, and Norfolk was definitely nautical. The idea was embraced, and the city cranked out 130 fiberglass mermaids for the ensuing event. The scaly women were designed to look like they were mid-swim, one arm outstretched in front, the other trailing back parallel to their flowing hair, with their fins kicked up so that their bodies formed the shape of a smile. Local businesses and artists transformed each one into a unique creation.

The Norfolk mermaids were so popular that they've since far exceeded those original 130, and the city is still manufacturing more today. More than that, the mermaid motif has expanded far beyond art installations in the city. Businesses brand themselves with the mermaid. Restaurants and bars offer mermaid-themed drinks. Gift shops are stuffed with mermaid merch. The creature is even incorporated into the city logo. Perhaps the most iconic of all the merfolk of Norfolk is the one in Town Point Park. It's the same shape as those original art installations, but is larger, made of metal, and installed as part of a fountain, with jets of water shooting up that seem to support the fish-woman.

Such is the power of monsters that you don't even need to see one to reap the resulting tourism and identity benefits. You just need to embrace one—of your choice.

– Woodbooger –

HOW TO MAKE A MONSTER

TYPE:	EARLIEST SIGHTING:
Humanoid	2011
LOCATION:	SIZE:
Norton, Virginia	7–8 feet tall

Sometimes the media makes the cryptid: a newspaper illustrator gives the monster its most identifiable form, or a journalist juices their story just enough to keep it interesting. And in cases where a cryptid is an outright hoax, the local newspaper editor should always be a prime suspect. But perhaps the strangest case of the media making a monster is the story of the woodbooger of Norton, Virginia.

In 2011, the Animal Planet channel television show *Finding Bigfoot* filmed an episode in southwestern Virginia called "Virginia Is for Bigfoot Lovers." Sure, Virginia has bigfoot sightings—every state has bigfoot sightings. But the town of Norton, near where the episode was filmed, claims no history, oral or otherwise, of the woodbooger (a regional term for bigfoot). In fact, according to the Bigfoot Field Researchers Organization website, not a single sighting of Virginia's total eighty-three has occurred in Wise County, where Norton is located.

Still, the episode of *Finding Bigfoot* opened by stating that accounts of woodboogers in the area go back centuries. The voiceover was augmented by aerial shots of thick, autumn-tinged forest foliage and flashes of yellow-tinted newspaper headlines that didn't come up in the searches I conducted. According to the show, the term woodbooger comes from the creature's propensity to sneak around and peek in on kids. This makes more sense than it might sound at first: *booger* is a variation on the term *bogey*, as in *bogeyman*, a catchall term for monster—particularly one used to frighten children. But the combination of *booger* and *woods* into *woodbooger* is unique.

The cast spent the show's runtime analyzing blurry footage of a dark form crossing a stream in front of an ATV and attempting to lure woodboogers in front of cameras with glazed donuts placed on tree limbs. They didn't find the woodbooger. (A common joke I've heard in cryptozoology circles is that after some dozen seasons of the show, *Finding Bigfoot* needs to be renamed *Not Finding Bigfoot*.)

An area that the team concentrated on was High Knob, one of the peaks of Stone Mountain, near Norton. The production visit and subsequent airing of the episode in early 2012 gave Norton a valuable opportunity: they could transform themselves into a Cryptid Town. Not only that, but in a culture where Bigfoot is basically a commodity, they could distinguish that commodity with a unique brand. Where else are you going to find something called a woodbooger?

The town got to work. Within a few years of the show's debut, Norton was officially sasquatch-friendly. They designated the Flag Rock Recreation Area of High Knob as a woodbooger sanctuary, putting up signs and painting giant footprints on the roads. They installed a six-foot-tall bigfoot statue. They jumpstarted an annual Woodbooger Festival, which happens every fall to this day. They even trademarked the term *woodbooger*. You can buy bigfoot merchandise anywhere, but you can only buy official Norton woodbooger merchandise from Norton.

One place you can't miss is Woodbooger Grill, a big-foot-themed eatery that doesn't stint on the woodbooger décor, inside or out. Be sure to order Woodbooger's Super Wood-burger: two patties, fried green tomato, fried pickles, BBQ pork, bacon, American cheese, shredded cheese, and cheese sauce. If you finish the whole thing in one sitting (including fries) they give you a T-shirt.

There are a lot of lessons for would-be Cryptid Towns here. One: you never know when a monster will strike, so when it does, capitalize on it fast. Two: find a way to differentiate your monster. Three: have fun with it!

– Rougarou –

CAJUN WEREWOLF

TYPE:	EARLIEST SIGHTING:
Humanoid-canine	18th century
LOCATION:	**SIZE:**
Southeast Louisiana	6–7 feet tall

"There are a lot of legends down here," says the clean-cut police officer to the camera. "Down here" is Terrebonne Parish, Louisiana, and the officer is one of the cast of the A&E channel reality show *Cajun Justice*, which follows officers from the local sheriff's office as they patrol their bit of the bayou. The officer concludes: "But probably the one that we get the most calls, of people saying that they've seen, would be the rougarou."

When the French left Louisiana in 1803 after the Louisiana Purchase, they left behind more than their cuisine, their language, and their religion. They left behind a monster: the loup-garou, which is the French word for werewolf. That name morphed delightfully the way words and customs do in the bayous of southeastern Louisiana and became rougarou, emphasis on the second syllable.

Often described as a wolf- or dog-headed human with glowing eyes (or sometimes more conventionally as a fully furred werewolf), the rougarou is less a cryptid encountered by eyewitnesses and more a boogeyman used to frighten children into acting right or avoiding dangerous areas of the swamp. It's also used as a warning for Catholics who don't abide by Lent (they can either become a rougarou or be killed by one). In the *Cajun Justice* episode, the rougarou manifested mostly in locals hearing growls near their chicken sheds and seeing shapes out in the marsh.

Still, you don't need to wade out into dark swamps or cheat during Lent to see a rougarou for yourself. Multiple towns and cities in southeastern Louisiana have elevated (and gentled) the monster into a symbol of local pride. Baton Rouge has a summer collegiate baseball team called the Rougarou, and the River Parishes Community College in Gonzalez also has a rougarou as its mascot. In the same Terrebonne Parish where *Cajun Justice* was filmed, the town of Houma is the center of all rougarou hullabaloo in the state, and wants you to know it as soon as you arrive. Behind the Houma Travel Center is an informational plaque that details some of the mysteries of the swamps, and one of those mysteries—along with pirate Jean Lafitte and ghost forests—is the rougarou. Houma is also home to the Rougarou Fest, a celebration of southeastern Louisiana folklore where people dress up as monsters, eat lots of food, and party at a parade. The mascot of the festival is a dancing Rougarou wearing a top hat, suit, and high-heeled boots. In 2019, Houma installed a permanent statue of the mascot downtown.

New Orleans is about sixty miles northeast of Houma. As one of the most famous cities in the country, it celebrates the rougarou in its own way. Its Audubon Zoo is a 58-acre expanse that is home to some 2,000 animals, including a rougarou. In the Louisiana Swamp exhibit, you'll find a glowing-eyed re-creation of the beast of the bayou. You can't talk about the swamp without talking about its monster, even at an auspicious scientific institution.

But one site in the French Quarter of New Orleans offers a dissenting opinion on the rougarou. Marie Laveau's House of Voodoo is a small museum packed with artifacts related to voodoo. It also recreates the rougarou, but not as a werewolf—its rougarou is a weregator. One of the exhibits displays a life-sized figure with the head of an alligator and the body (and khaki shirt) of a man. A placard beside it calls the creature a cross between a French werewolf, an African vampire, and a voodoo zombie. It claims that it can steal your soul with its eyes, that throwing salt on it will make it combust, and that every St. John's Eve (June 23), all the rougarou in the state gather on the banks of the Bayou Goula for what's called Bal Goula, a rougarou bash where they all get together to dance in the moonlight, although probably not in top hats and high-heeled boots.

Whether wolfman or alligator-man, the important warning here is that there are swamp things in southeastern Louisiana that are a lot more fun to meet in the broad daylight of a community festival than by yourself in the dark sogginess of the bayou.

❮❯ ◆ ❯❯

– Chupacabra –

GOATSUCKING GARGOYLE

TYPE:	EARLIEST SIGHTING:
Reptilian or canine	1995
LOCATION:	**SIZE:**
Morovis and Orocovis, Puerto Rico; Southern US, particularly Texas	3–4 feet tall

The chupacabra crept onto the cryptid scene relatively recently—it's a nineties kid—but the creature's popularity rose fast. Internet-speeds fast. There were only two years between its first sighting and an *X-Files* episode about the beast (season four, episode eleven, entitled "El Mundo Gira"). It was almost like there was a vacant cryptozoological niche waiting for the right creature to slot into it. *Something* had to suck the goats.

The chupacabra is described as a three-to-four-foot-tall reptilian creature with a hunched shape similar to a kangaroo, sharp fangs not at all similar to a kangaroo, glowing red eyes, and a row of spikes down its back. It might be furred, or it might be scaly. Some even say it looks awfully similar to classic gray aliens with their domed heads and large eyes. The primary evidence of the existence of chupacabras is their victims: dead, exsanguinated farm animals with puncture wounds in their hides, as if their blood had been sucked out of them by desperate vampires. And that's where the cryptid gets its name: chupacabra is Spanish for goatsucker.

The gargoyle-like creature—and the dead farm animals—first appeared in Puerto Rico in 1995. The sightings began in the middle of the island, near the towns of Morovis and Orocovis, and spread throughout the territory from there. Over the course of 1995 and 1996, some 2,000 small animal deaths were attributed to the chupacabra (or chupacabras) in Puerto Rico. Its victims included calves, sheep, dogs, pigs, geese, chickens, turkeys, rabbits, and of course goats.

Human encounters with the monster itself were brief and mostly consisted of glimpses of the creature as it scampered off after feeding. In the town of Canovanas, Mayor José Soto organized multiple hunting parties to find it. "People here are frightened," he told Reuters. Researchers looked deeper into the records and uncovered a similar event that had happened two decades previous, in 1975, in the town of Moca. The bodies of cows, chickens, and goats were found drained of blood. Back then, they called the creature the Moca Vampire.

Soon, Spanish TV picked up the chupacabra story, as did the eager blogs and forums and rudimentary news sites of the burgeoning internet. Eventually, sightings of the creature spread across Latin America and into southern US states like Florida, Arizona, and Texas. When chupacabra sightings began springing up in the US, and more specifically Texas, something weird happened. The chupacabra changed. Descriptions of it morphed from an alien vampire kangaroo to . . . a hairless blue dog. The term chupacabra started being applied to strange, bluish, sickly looking canines that farmers and ranchers would find attacking their animals. These creatures started appearing so often that they shouldered out the Puerto Rican form of the cryptid in the news headlines. The canine form of chupacabra turned out to be less savvy than its predecessor (and most cryptids), as it was not only a lot easier to witness and capture on film, but a lot easier to catch.

There have been enough killed that we have taxidermied specimens. And these bald blue dog attacks are still happening today, three decades after chupacabra was added to the cryptozoolexicon. Every so often a hairless, blue canine is shot (by camera or shotgun) while attacking somebody's chickens or goats and gets famous. Sure, debunkers yell something about mange and other skin diseases that cause animals to look like zombie dogs, but that doesn't change the fact that these Texas blue dogs, unlike any other cryptid, leave their corpses behind. And those corpses, once taxidermied, goes on tour to various small museums.

For a more permanent installation, look no further than a couple of Texas zoos. In 2020, the San Antonio Zoo unveiled a chupacabra exhibit, where visitors can witness chupacabras in their native habitat. The statues of the creatures are outright terrifying: brown, four-legged monsters with multiple rows of spines down their backs and tiny black eyes and bulbous growths on their flanks. About 300 miles east in the Kingdom Zoo Wildlife Center in Orange is another chupacabra exhibit. The statue at that small facility depicts a bald coyote with long fangs and a mohawk of hair from crown to tail. But whether it's a Texas blue dog or a Puerto Rican goatsucker or a Moca Vampire, they all answer to chupacabra.

Movie Monsters

California is credited with introducing the world to bigfoot. It might also be responsible for introducing the world to lots of other cryptids, too. That is, if you believe the skeptics … and the power of cinema.

The first sighting of a chupacabra was in August 1995, by Madelyne Tolentino. She described (and sketched) the thing that had been killing livestock in Puerto Rico as a spiky-backed alien-like creature with thin limbs. The sighting occurred a month after the science fiction/horror movie *Species* came out, which also starred a spiky-backed alien creature with thin limbs. In a later interview, Tolentino admitted to having watched the movie weeks before the sighting.

The Wolf Woman of Mobile, Alabama—a human-faced canid creature that walked on all fours—was reported to the local newspaper in April 1971. At the same time, trailers were running on TV and theater screens for a movie called *The Mephisto Waltz*. The surreal trailer prominently features an eerie scene in which a dog walks around wearing a mask of a human face over its head.

It works the other way around, too. Cryptids—and former cryptids—have inspired countless movies. The coelacanth was a massive fish thought to be extinct for sixty-five million years—until a living specimen was caught in 1938 off the coast of South Africa. It inspired screenwriter Arthur Ross to write a movie about a prehistoric fish creature that had survived into modern times: *The Creature from the Black Lagoon*. It even goes full circle, because *The Creature from the Black Lagoon*, which came out in 1954, is also believed to have influenced the 1955 sighting of the Loveland Frogmen of Ohio.

If "you just imagined it" is the worst thing you can say to a cryptid witness, maybe the second worst is, "oh, I saw that movie."

— Minnesota Iceman —

A MIDWESTERN MONSTER DOWN SOUTH

TYPE:	EARLIEST SIGHTING:
Humanoid	1960s
LOCATION:	**NOTABLE FEATURE:**
Austin, Texas	Frozen in ice

The Museum of the Weird in Austin, Texas, is a P. T. Barnum-haunted carnival celebration of the macabre and the monstrous. Inside is a joyful aggregation of movie monsters, skeletons, mummies, freakshow performers both alive and dead, and, of course, cryptids. Inside are multiple statues of bigfoot, along with footprint casts. There's an original photo of the Cottingley Fairies, one of a set of hoax photos created by two girls, aged nine and sixteen, that fascinated and fooled early twentieth century England. There's a mounted jackalope head, a fur-bearing a trout (a fish covered in white fur so thick it'd make a yeti jealous), and plenty of FeeJee mermaids (the half-monkey, half-fish taxidermy gaffs that no museum of the strange would be complete without). It also showcases one of the most infamous cryptozoological oddities in the country, one that's an even bigger hoax than a fish-monkey, fur-fish, horned rabbit, and paper fairy combined. This Texas museum owns the Minnesota Iceman.

The Minnesota Iceman is a dark-furred, prehistoric-looking wildman corpse frozen in a coffin of ice. Its position is prostrate, on its back, with one large hand on its stomach and the other held over its head like it's waving to someone in the far distance. One of its eyes dangles grotesquely from its socket. The creature was toured around the country in the 1960s and 1970s by a man named Frank Hansen, who displayed it at carnivals and fairs as the "Siberskoye Creature." Hansen claimed it was owned by a California millionaire whose name he had to keep secret (leading some to believe it was Jimmy Stewart, who years earlier had helped smuggle a yeti finger into England via his wife's lingerie case). As to the supposed origin story, it had a few, from being found floating in the icy ocean off Siberia to being discovered in a freezer in Hong Kong to being shot during a hunting trip in Minnesota, where Hansen was from. Eventually, it caught the attention of founding father cryptozoologists Ivan T. Sanderson and Bernard Heuvelmans, who examined it in 1968 in Minnesota, where it got its forever name of Minnesota Iceman.

These two men were enamored of the creature and bought into its validity as the holy grail of cryptozoology: a cryptid corpse. They gave it a scientific name, *Homo pongoides*, wrote about it for a scientific journal, and staunchly defended it against the barbs of skeptics. However, when a primatologist at the Smithsonian Institution pointed out that the Minnesota Iceman was obviously a latex dummy, Hansen backpedaled. He explained that of course it was a latex dummy. It was a replica he had made to replace the authentic body that Sanderson and Heuvelmans had examined originally. Hansen claimed he had performed the switch because its original owner wanted it back. But he couldn't or wouldn't produce the real body, nor name the millionaire owner, and most saw through the veneer.

After that, the facsimile disappeared just as mysteriously as the supposed original body. For decades, nobody knew where it was, until one day in 2013 it popped up on eBay and was scooped up by Steve and Veronica Busti, owners of the Museum of the Weird, and put on display. The latex lie was an important find, not just for the history of cryptozoology, but for Steve Busti personally. He had seen the Iceman when it originally traveled back in the seventies, toward the end of its tour. Busti was five, and his aunt took him to see it where it was displayed in a truck in a Kmart parking lot.

Seeing the weird wonder in ice had a large impact on the small boy. In an interview posted on YouTube with bigfoot enthusiast J. R. Bob Dobbs Jr., Busti says, "Had I not seen this, I can honestly say, we wouldn't be here today because there probably wouldn't be a Museum of the Weird." And who knows—perhaps kids wandering the Museum of the Weird today will say something similar when they grow up.

Pascagoula Elephant Man

INTERGALACTIC CATCH AND RELEASE

TYPE:	**EARLIEST SIGHTING:**
Alien	1973
LOCATION:	**SIZE:**
Pascagoula, Mississippi	5 feet tall

Fishermen are known to tell tall tales, but the tale that Charles Hickson and Calvin Parker Jr. told of the night of October 11, 1973, in Pascagoula, Mississippi, is a bit taller than most. Five feet tall—with elephant skin and carrot ears.

The two men—Hickson, forty-two, and Parker, nineteen—worked together at the Wagner Shipyard. They decided one evening to head to the East Pascagoula River near the shipyard to do some fishing. No sooner had they dropped bait than they heard a hiss or zipper sound and an oblong craft with flashing blue lights appeared, hovering two feet off the ground. The lights were so bright they couldn't tell exactly how big the strange object was. But they would soon find out that it was at least big enough for five people. Well, two people and three monsters. Hickson and Parker were about to get their membership card for what was, at the time, a burgeoning club of people: alien abductees.

But here is what separates their abduction story from so many others and why the Pascagoula Elephant Men are often lumped into cryptozoology texts: the description of the three

creatures that exited that craft is bonkers and unlike any creature ever described in history or fantasy. They were five feet tall, and robotic in that they didn't seem to move organically—or at all, other than their arms. They had wrinkly gray elephantine skin, lobster claws for hands, legs fused into a column, no eyes, slits for a mouth, and "carrot-like" appendages jutting out the front and sides of their heads in place of noses and ears—like those rubber Panic Pete toys whose eyes, ears, and nose extend on stalks when squeezed.

Both men felt paralyzed. They could only watch in silent, motionless terror as the three creatures glided over to them on those pillar-like lower extremities. Neither man put up a fight as they were taken by their arms, lifted, and levitated inside the craft. There, they were scanned from head to toe by an eyeball the size of a football. In 2018, Parker would go into more detail, stating that a small object flew around his head making clicking noises, and that a feminine creature completely unlike the Elephant Men inserted a finger down his throat until he choked. She then assured him through mental telepathy that he and Hickson were safe.

After the strange examination, the men were released, with nothing to show for their experience except for some empty fishhooks and a whopper of a story that nobody would ever believe. Still, Hickson and Parker had to try. They couldn't pretend it didn't happen. It was too weird—sanity-shaking. Plus, in the words of Hickson to the *Clarion Ledger*, "what if it's a threat to our country?" The two men sat in the car, took a few hits of whiskey, and contacted the nearby Keesler Air Force Base, which referred them to the police. The police took down their story and then tried to determine if the men were lying by leaving them alone in a room while secretly recording them.

Hickson and Parker didn't so much as wink at each other. Transcriptions of their conversation revealed two men who were extremely shaken by what they had experienced.

Over the decades, most of the details of this story were relayed by the elder Hickson, who told it to anybody with non-carrot ears—UFO conventions, newspapers, television shows—right up until his death in 2011. Parker disappeared for decades, but granted some interviews in the 2010s. In 2018 and 2019, he released a pair of books about his experiences: *Pascagoula—The Closest Encounter: My Story* and *Pascagoula—The Story Continues: New Evidence and New Witnesses*.

In a world where the predominant alien sightings are of the short, big-headed, bug-eyed gray sort, who would take floaty carrot-headed creatures seriously? Well, it took them almost half a century, but the city of Pascagoula and its historical society finally did. In 2019, eight years after Hickson's death and forty-six years after the encounter, they unveiled a historic placard on the bank of the East Pascagoula in Lighthouse Park near where the encounter happened. It briefly tells the story and features an artist's depiction of the Elephant Men. Calvin Parker Jr. and the family of Charles Hickson were in attendance. I have only one complaint: the placard completely misses the opportunity to tell a joke about fishermen finding themselves the subjects of an intergalactic catch-and-release program.

– Wolf Woman –

PRETTY HAIRY

TYPE:	EARLIEST SIGHTING:
Canine-humanoid	1971
LOCATION:	**NOTABLE FEATURE:**
Mobile, Alabama	Human female torso and head, lupine body

Sometimes cryptozoology is a real Mongolian Death-worm fest. And I'm not referring to the gender spectrum of cryptozoologists (although that's probably true, too)—I mean the cryptids themselves. There are lizard-men and dog-men and elephant-men and moth-men and goat-men and bunny-men, but precious few hyphen women of any kind. Sure, the bigfoot in the Patterson-Gimlin footage has breasts and, sure, the mermaids of Norfolk are female, but female cryptids still beat their wings, moth-woman-like, against a glass ceiling. That's why the Wolf Woman of Mobile stands out and should be celebrated by her home state of Alabama.

Some might describe the Wolf Woman of Mobile as a top-less woman in shaggy pants, but not the terrified populace of Mobile. In early April 1971, witnesses in that city called the police and the newspapers for two solid weeks with panicked tales of a half woman, half wolf prowling the night.

The story first surfaced in the *Mobile Register* on April 8, which over the course of the previous week had received some fifty calls from terrified people who had either seen or heard about a wolf-woman prowling Davis Avenue (now Dr. Martin Luther King Jr. Avenue) and the Plateau area, a historic and predominantly Black area of the city also known as Africatown. One unnamed teenager reported: "My daddy saw it down in a marsh and it chased him home. Now, my mommy keeps all the doors and windows locked." The wolf woman was described as hairy, as half woman and half wolf, and also—bizarrely—as pretty, which might be a clue as to which half of her was woman.

And then the story got what it really needed to stick in people's imaginations: an artist's conception. If you can't get a blurry photo of a cryptid, you need a witness drawing of a cryptid, and if you can't get either one of those, you need the newspaper that breaks the story to illustrate it. And the *Mobile Press Register* did exactly that. The unnamed artist drew the beast on all fours—despite none of the recorded reports stating that—and very much unlike the classic dog-men and werewolf stories in which their bipedal form is an important part of

their otherworldliness. But, woman, what an illustration—like, town-seal worthy. It shows a creature with the body of a wolf, hair from neck to tail, on all clawed fours, and with a twist. It's topped by a woman's head with pointy ears, a five o'clock shadow, a long, straight hairdo that looks fresh from the salon, and human breasts. It's Morticia Addams mixed with Cousin Itt: pretty *and* hairy.

And while the she-wolf never appeared again in the city of Mobile, I can't close this entry with a better line than this one from the original *Mobile Register* article: "Paris had its Hunchback of Notre Dame. Maybe Mobile has its Wolf Woman of Davis Avenue." Now if only Mobile would add this gorgeous wolf woman to the town seal.

— Tennessee Terror —

CRYPTID WITH A CURSE

TYPE:	EARLIEST SIGHTING:
Aquatic	1822
LOCATION:	**SIZE:**
Tennessee River, Tennessee	25 feet long

Cryptids, for all their scary monsterhood, rarely hurt people. But they always seem like they want to—they come at you in the night with large fangs and big claws, giant hairy muscles, sharp beaks and horns, and spikes on their backs and tails. But the Tennessee Terror, while in most ways a typical aquatic cryptid, has a unique method of harm. You die whether it swallows you whole or not. Because it's cursed.

The Tennessee Terror is serpentine, twenty-five feet long, with a spiny back from which extends a two-foot-long black fin and a giant canine-like head. It lurks in the Tennessee River, although sometimes it'll head up a tributary or two. The origin of the curse it bears is unknown, but it's said that just seeing the monster is enough to invoke it, causing the witness to die in a year or less.

The monster is primarily sourced to the work of contemporary historian and author E. Randall Floyd. The story he tells in the *Spartanburg Herald-Journal* of South Carolina (among other places) begins in 1822 when a Tennessee farmer named Buck Sutton was fishing from the shore of the Tennessee River at a place called Van's Hole. Something dark and serpentine splashing in the water caught his attention—something his rod was no match for. A fish Sutton would later describe to his friends as "monstrous" was causing a commotion in the shallows about thirty feet from where he stood. He left the spot immediately, not with terror or excitement, but with sadness. He somehow knew what that thing was and knew he was cursed for seeing it. Sutton died a few days later of causes unrecorded—or as the first victim of the Tennessee Terror.

In 1827, the Tennessee Terror was spotted again by a man named Billy Burns. Burns described it as a blue-yellow "snake-like thing" at least as long as the canoe he was in (or almost out of, as the monster nearly capsized it). According to Floyd, the *Chattanooga Daily Chronicle* reported that Burns died a year later "in some strange manner."

In 1829, a farmer named Jim Windom was fishing in a boat when he saw the creature's head emerge from the water not ten feet away. "It slowly passed me, then rolled over on its side," he said, according to Floyd. It swam around his boat a few times, and Windom saw the black fin jutting from the water. He paddled furiously to the safety of dry land, although he knew that safety would be short lived. He had seen the fish, and he was now cursed. Windom died a few months later of fever, despite trying to fight the curse by going to church and praying daily.

Floyd claims that as the river got choppy with steamboats, sightings of the monster became more rare. And as the Tennessee Terror was seen less and less, the curse also seemed to lose power. A few people would spot it in the mid-1930s without ill effects. A woman named Sallie Wilson saw it multiple times in the river, and the last sighting recorded was by her husband, J. C. Wilson. He spotted the creature cavorting in the water "in a playful mood." The husband and wife did fine after that.

These days, fishers on the Tennessee River don't talk about the Tennessee Terror much. If they talk about a monster in the river at all, it will usually be Catzilla, a giant catfish the size of a Volkswagen Bug that swallows unlucky divers. However, this story is as common throughout the country as catfish themselves. But only the Tennessee Terror is cursed, and that's worth commemorating.

– Hopkinsville Goblin –

GUNFIGHT AT THE E.T. CORRAL

TYPE:	EARLIEST SIGHTING:
Alien-humanoid	1955
LOCATION:	**SIZE:**
Hopkinsville, Kentucky	3–4 feet tall

Elmer Sutton and Billy Ray Taylor met while working on the carnival circuit. When Taylor and his wife visited Sutton at his family farm on August 21, 1955, somewhere between Hopkinsville and Kelly, Kentucky, they were ready to hang out and play some card games. Instead, they endured a night of weirdness that no career in the carnival could have prepared them for. The event that has come to be known as the Kelly-Hopkinsville Encounter is more a chapter of ufology than cryptozoology. It even popularized the term "little green men." But how can I write a book about monsters in America and ignore three-foot-tall goblins? I can't.

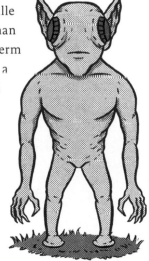

Of course, the Kelly-Hopkinsville Encounter wasn't so much an encounter. It was a battle. On that summer night, about a dozen people were at the farm, seven of whom were children. Taylor went out to the well after dark to get water and witnessed a round, metallic object in the sky, trailing light. He went back inside the house and told everybody what he had seen, but nobody believed him. That is, until a monster appeared in the darkness at their front door. It was short, three or four feet tall, with large yellow eyes set about six inches apart and tall sharp ears. Its arms were overly long and clawed, and its skin seemed to glow with a silvery hue. Taylor grabbed a gun and made first contact with the deadly end, but the silver goblin merely floated away. Stepping outside to make sense of the situation, Taylor was immediately accosted by a pair of claws extending from the roof. Somebody grabbed Taylor and pulled him inside, and one of the other family members shot at the thing.

The creatures kept coming, up to fifteen of them, and the besieged carnival workers and their families barricaded themselves inside the house for an old-fashioned shoot-out. The creatures scrabbled at the windows, perched in trees, and clattered about on the roof, while the families continued to take shots. Whenever it seemed like they had hit one of the creatures, the goblin would float away, as if the family was playing a rigged carnival game.

After four hours of this horror movie, the Taylors and the Suttons made a mad dash to their cars and drove to Hopkinsville to tell the police about these "little silver men." The police came out there (along with some investigators from the nearby Fort Campbell army base) but didn't find even so much as a trail of glowing alien blood. Instead, they found a farm that had been shot to pieces by terrestrial bullets.

The authorities soon left, and the Taylors and Suttons tried to at least get a few hours of sleep after their night of terror. But then, around three in the morning, the creatures returned. That standoff, which was more a vigil than a battle, lasted until day-break, when the nightmare finally ended. Or was replaced by another one.

The next day the property was crawling with tourists and investigators. Many in the town found the story humorous, joking that the farm had been the victim of monkeys from a passing circus. Others heckled the cops who had investigated the night before with, "Seen any little men today?" Newspapers across the country picked up the story, and the description of the goblins telephone-gamed into "little green men," a phrase that up to that point had only been used in science fiction.

Less than two weeks after the incident, the Suttons moved away, annoyed and frustrated by the ridicule. According to Elmer Sutton's daughter Geraldine Sutton-Stith (who wasn't born at the time of the encounter but would go on to write multiple books about it), her father harbored a lot of anger and resentment at not being believed. He even regretted going to the police station that night.

But what Sutton wouldn't live to see—that might have made him feel a little better—was the Little Green Men Days festival (although he'd probably tire of repeating to everyone, "they weren't green!"). In 2010, Kelly kicked off an annual commemoration of that night of terror, drawing tourists to town with alien-themed costume contests, rides, and games.

Eventually, an annual festival wasn't enough for the residents of Kelly. To memorialize the incident year-round, they erected a flying saucer at Kelley Station Park, a location that's only a quarter mile from the site of the original attack. That way nobody will ever forget the first intergalactic battle in the history of the planet.

–Pope Lick Monster –

DEADLY TRACKS

TYPE:	EARLIEST SIGHTING:
Mammalian-humanoid	1960s
LOCATION:	**NOTABLE FEATURE:**
Louisville, Kentucky	Lives under railroad trestle

The Pope Lick Monster of Louisville, Kentucky, is not itself celebrated, commemorated, or memorialized. It's feared, even by those who don't believe it exists. However, the creature is inextricably linked to a specific object in Louisville, one that draws visitors to the monster as effectively as a historical plaque or statue: a train trestle bridge.

The train trestle was built in the late nineteenth century and is owned by the Norfolk Southern Railway. It passes over Pope Lick Creek and South Pope Lick Road at the edge of the Rolleigh Peterson Educational Forest in eastern Louisville. At its highest, the 772-foot-long trestle is a deadly ninety feet above the ground. It looks abandoned and rickety, but some two dozen freight trains cross it each day. And that's not the only thing dangerous about the bridge.

The Pope Lick Monster is said to live under the trestle like the troll in the Three Billy Goats Gruff fairytale. The beast is a Kentucky-fried version of the Greek satyr, a goat-human hybrid, although some sources describe the monster as half sheep, half human. It's often depicted by artists as a bipedal, furry human-oid with a goat's face and curving ram's horns, although in some accounts the monster is headless, as if its head had been severed at the neck by the wheels of a locomotive.

But the trestle isn't just the home of the Pope Lick Monster: it's also the monster's murder weapon. The goatman lures people onto the trestle by either hypnotizing them or mimicking human voices. Once the victim finds themselves trapped atop the vertiginous bridge, they are killed either by oncoming trains or by the long drop to the ground below. Even driving underneath the bridge is dangerous, as the Pope Lick Monster has been said to drop from the trestle to attack cars.

But the thing about this monster is that, even though it may only exist in the realm of urban legend, it has caused real deaths. Every couple of years somebody dies on that bridge. Trains are often unable to stop in time, and anybody who finds themselves on the tracks at the wrong moment will have nowhere to go but under the wheels of the train or off the side of the bridge. Tragically, these deaths are often of people who went atop the bridge looking for the Pope Lick Monster, making them actual victims of the creature.

The last victim on record died in May 2019. Two

teenage girls, one fifteen and one sixteen, were on the tracks when a train crossed. One was killed immediately, and the other survived after being taken to the hospital in critical condition. Whether they were up there looking for a monster is uncertain, but probable: part of the legend holds that walking across the bridge can summon the monster.

But another death three years earlier was more directly connected to the Pope Lick Monster. In April 2016, two Ohio tourists, twenty-six-year-old Roquel Bain and her boyfriend, forty-one-year-old David Knee, were on their way to the Waverly Hills Sanatorium in Louisville, a famous destination for those who like to ghost hunt or explore spooky, abandoned sites. Before heading to the asylum, they decided to check out the infamous Pope Lick Monster bridge. When the train came speeding across the trestle, Bain was hit by the train and fell to her death, while Knee was able to survive by wrapping his arms and legs around the edge of the bridge. He was barely able to hold on as the structure vibrated ferociously.

You can see why local authorities try to keep people away. A trail beneath the bridge is safe (unless the goatman jumps off the bridge onto you), but authorities have fenced off the entrance to the bridge, festooning it with NO TRESPASSING signs. There are criminal penalties for interfering with the railroad.

Beyond the other benefits of memorializing one's local monsters, there's a safety reason to erect a plaque or statue dedicated to the Pope Lick goatman—and Louisville should place it as far as they can from the terrors of the trestle.

—Oklahoma Octopus—

NEW SQUID ON THE BLOCK

TYPE:	EARLIEST SIGHTING:
Aquatic	Early 2000s
LOCATION:	**SIZE:**
Northeast Oklahoma	20 feet long

Oh, did Oklahoma zag while everyone else zigged with their aquatic cryptids. The people of Oklahoma didn't jump on the plesiosaur bandwagon, didn't get entangled with anything humpy or serpentine. Instead they asked: "What's the coolest thing in the ocean? We want that for our lake monster." And that, of course, is the octopus. Octopuses are such bizarre creatures that some have suggested that the seeds of their evolution were deposited on Earth via meteorites from outer space. You have to be a pretty cool animal to get that kind of backstory. Plus, Oklahoma Octopus alliterates, which is extremely important in marketing cryptids.

Freshwater octopuses in general are considered cryptids since all known octopus species are saltwater denizens. Every once in a while, someone will find a small octopus while fishing in a stream or a lake, but these situations are often pranks or involve naively released pets or fishing bait. However they get there, these freshwater octopuses quickly die. But not the Oklahoma Octopus—or, as I and nobody else like to call it, Ock-ock. Ock-ock is reddish-brown, with leathery skin, and is about twenty feet long. By comparison, the largest non-cryptid octopus in the world is the giant Pacific octopus, which averages sixteen feet and maxes out at 110 pounds (although according to *National Geographic*, a record-breaking specimen reached a whopping thirty feet long and 600 pounds).

The main evidence of the existence of Ock-ock isn't old newspaper accounts of sightings or Native American stories of magical beasts. In fact, the freshwater octopus has never been seen—by anyone who survived the encounter, at least. But it has been blamed for the many drowning deaths in Oklahoma's many lakes—and I do mean "lakes" plural. Because yet another way that Oklahoma zagged with its cryptid was to assign it to not just one lake, but three: Thunderbird Lake, Oolagah Lake, and Tenkiller Ferry Lake, which form a triangle in the northwest corner of the state. Whether that means there are multiple Oklahoma Octopuses or one that just gets around is uncertain. The only bit of physical evidence that's been produced is an octopus the size of a human hand that was found dead by fishermen in Tenkiller Ferry Lake in June 2020.

The Oklahoma Octopus is a very new cryptid story, with sources going back only fifteen years or so. The earliest account I can find is a single paragraph in a 2007 book called *The Monster Spotter's Guide to North America* by Scott Francis. Most references to the creature can be traced back to an episode of Animal Planet's faux-found-footage series *Lost Tapes* from 2009. Ock-ock being a new lake monster makes sense, though, because the lakes of Oklahoma are also quite new. Oklahoma claims about 200 lakes, most of which are human made (including all the large ones). That's more than any other state. And all three lakes that are said to hide Ock-ock are artificial. Thunderbird Lake was created in the 1960s, Oolagah in 1950, and Tenkiller Ferry in the late 1940s to early 1950s.

Although stories about the Oklahoma Octopus are quite recent, I did find a reference to an octopus in Oklahoma from 1927. The *Democrat-American* out of Sallislaw, Oklahoma, tells the story of three men—Tim Ross, J. V. Sellers, and Rayford McAlpine—fishing at Lee Creek, which is mostly in Arkansas but bends into Oklahoma, and isn't too far from where Tenkiller Ferry Lake would eventually be. They claimed to see a disturbance in the water like an "oil well boiling." Looking closer, they determined it was an octopus inking the water to a radius of ten feet. The account ends with a warning to anybody fishing or swimming in the area: "be on the lookout for the spiderlike fish and avoid the vicinity."

A warning like that would make a good sign on the banks of these lakes, maybe even as a creative way to educate people on the dangers of drowning. Ock-ock could be a mascot for swimming and boating safety. If you have a cryptid as unique, alliterative, and with as cool a nickname as Ock-ock, you should put it to work for you.

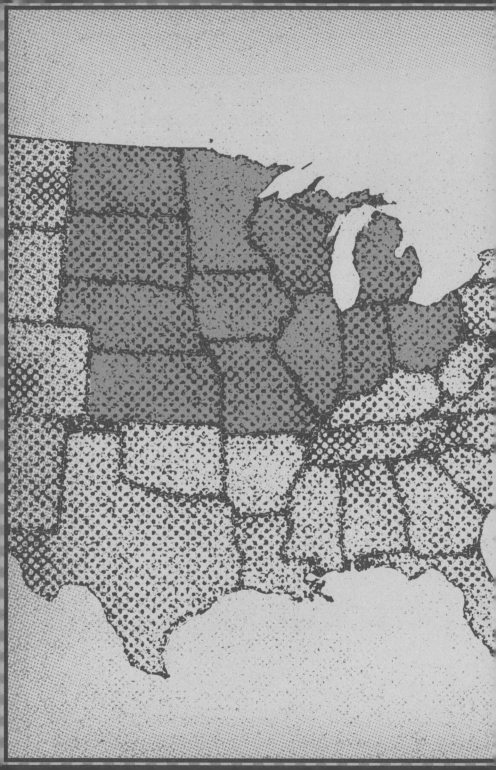

PART III:
THE MIDWEST

The Midwest is the least populous region of the country, which means more room for those shy cryptids to roam. And, man, do they roam the dark heartland of the United States of America. Few states can boast the sheer volume and variety of monsters that Wisconsin does, or Illinois, or Ohio. And you'll find some doozies in these wide flatlands, including monster birds, werewolves galore, and all manner of horned and spiky cryptids. Now you know why they call it flyover country: you have to get through it as fast as possible. Or else.

–Enfield Monster –

SCRATCHES IN THE NIGHT

TYPE:	EARLIEST SIGHTING:
Mammalian	1973
LOCATION:	SIZE:
Enfield, Illinois	4–5 feet tall

You're a kid. It's nighttime. Mom and Dad are out. Suddenly, you hear a scratching outside your house. It stops. You hear it at a different part of the house. It stops again. Then it scratches on your front door. It's an absolute nightmare straight out of an Alvin Schwartz book. But that's how the tale of the Enfield Monster begins, a creature that terrorized the town of Enfield, Illinois, for two weeks in the spring of 1973. Well, that's not quite true. It terrorized one family. The rest of the town was generally amused by it.

When Henry McDaniel, a fifty-year-old World War II veteran, returned home with his wife on April 25 at around 9:30 p.m., they found their children terrified. Something had been scratching around the house. Turns out, it wasn't done, either. Soon, McDaniel heard it too, at the front door. It was trying to get inside. Thinking it might be a bear, McDaniel grabbed his .22 and a flashlight and opened the door. The scratcher was about a dozen feet away and like nothing he'd ever seen.

He described it as four or five feet tall, with an almost humanoid body covered in grayish fur. It had stubby arms, large pink eyes the size of flashlight lenses, and three legs. It would come to be called the Enfield Monster (or, alternately, the Enfield Horror). The creature hissed and took off in fast, giant leaps on those three legs across McDaniel's lawn and the train tracks beyond and into the darkness. McDaniel squeezed off four shots. "When I fired that first shot, I know I hit it," he later told the Associated Press.

I know what you're thinking: kangaroo. Kangaroos are also gray and bouncy with small arms, and the third "leg" is its tail, right? Not so fast. That's exactly what everybody else thought, too. But McDaniel claimed that he knew very well what a kangaroo looked like (and what it didn't look like). He'd kept one as a pet during his Army days while stationed in Australia.

McDaniel called the police, but by the time they arrived, the only evidence of the bizarre visitor was a scratched-up screen window, some hair in the bushes, and pawprints that would later be described as either five- or six-toed. A pet store owner named Ed Phillips came out and verified the tracks, as well. "It couldn't be a hoax," he told the United Press International, noting how some tracks were hidden in dense brush.

As newspapers got ahold of the story, the world seemed to descend on the tiny town of Enfield, much to the chagrin of White County Sheriff Roy Poshard Jr. He was the one who had to deal with the crowds; he even had to throw a few people in jail. He incarcerated five men who were wandering the woods carting

rifles. They claimed to have shot at something they described as grayish and running faster than a person could. He booked them on the charge of hunting outside of season. No exceptions for cryptids.

Among the curiosity seekers and monster hunters that the sighting attracted was a young anthropology student from the University of Illinois, who recorded a strange screech that he heard in the forest. His name was Loren Coleman, future founder of the International Cryptozoology Museum in Portland, Maine (see page 38). Others got closer encounters. On May 6, a radio director named Rick Rainbow (of WWKI in Kokomo, Indiana, which was about four hours northeast of Enfield) came down and went looking for the Enfield monster with some friends. They claimed to have found it in an abandoned shed near McDaniel's property. It was a gray, stooped thing that ran into the night and made a screeching noise.

Meanwhile, even though out-of-towners were in love with the beast, most of the townies didn't believe McDaniel at all, which infuriated him. He's quoted by the Capital News Service as saying, "There's other people that seen it, too. They just ain't sayin' anything." But McDaniel did finally receive a bit of closure. On the night of May 6, the same night Rick Rainbow had his sighting, McDaniel had yet another encounter. Sometime around three a.m., the noise of dogs baying pulled him from sleep and he ventured outside. He saw the Enfield Monster walking slowly along the train tracks. He didn't try to shoot it this time. He told the Associated Press, "If they do find it, they will find more than one and they won't be from this planet."

So maybe it was an unclassified creature from this planet or another. Or maybe it fits into the category of devil monkeys and phantom kangaroos that riddle cryptozoology. Either way, the

Enfield Monster is worth recognizing in some public way. At least as a warning. If you ever hear a scratching on your door at night, maybe don't open it, else you might turn your town into a Cryptid Town.

Actually, for my sake, please open it.

– Piasa Bird –

MISSISSIPPI MONSTER MURAL

TYPE:	EARLIEST SIGHTING:
Aerial	Prehistory
LOCATION:	**SIZE:**
Alton, Illinois	48 feet long

At my back was the Mississippi River, a natural wonder that should never be at one's back. But what distracted me from it was the massive cave, the entrance of which was four stories tall, looming over me like it was Godzilla's lair. But I was in Alton, Illinois, not usually considered a kaiju home base. Then I saw the monster.

It was the size of a bus, gold and scaly with red wings. It was vaguely lion-shaped, with wicked talons for feet, thorny antlers atop its head, and a face with bright red lips slashed by two stalagmite fangs in its lower, bearded jaw. Around it wrapped a long, ropey tail, segmented like a scorpion's but ending in paired fins like a fish's tail. The beast looked like some sort of strange dragon, and it kind of was: a Native American—possibly Mississippian—creature called the Piasa Bird. Fortunately, it wasn't slavering hungrily fifty feet above me. It was painted on the rough rock wall beside the cave, a monster mural above the Mississippi.

In 1673, the French Jesuit priest and explorer Jacques Marquette recorded a painting of two monsters on a bluff overlooking the Mississippi. He described the scaly creatures as the size of calves, with deer horns, red eyes, tiger's beards, men's faces, and long tails that wrapped around them and ended in fish fins. The painting was in green, red, and black. In other words, it was similar to the mural I was admiring on that bluff outside of Alton—minus a few details, including the wings.

By the beginning of the eighteenth century, the painting Marquette saw had vanished. By the end of the nineteenth century, the bluff itself followed, quarried away by a limestone company. But the Piasa Bird wasn't forgotten. Over the decades, it was resurrected numerous times. In the early twentieth century, an artist repainted it on a bluff a couple hundred yards upstream from the original location. The bluff was another limestone quarry site, its insides conveniently hollowed into a monster cave. Eventually, that mural went the way of the previous Piasa Bird. In the 1980s, the town bolted a metal panel with the Piasa Bird painted on it to the bluff face, but the panel rusted and was removed. It was eventually refurbished and put to use at a high school sports field north of Alton, in the town of Piasa. (Piasa's high school mascot is the Piasa Bird; Alton's high school mascot is a redbird.) In 1998, local artist Dave Stevens repainted the current incarnation of the beast on the bluff, and these days it gets a regular fresh coat.

For years, the story of this beast was sourced to an account published in the *Family Magazine* in 1836 by a minister and professor named John Russell. It was this piece that gave the creature the name Piasa (which Russell said was an Illinois word meaning "bird that devours men"). Russell's article tells the story of a man-eating monster that lived in a cave and a Native American hero named Ouatoga who, at the direction of the Great Spirit, ambushed and killed the Piasa Bird by concealing twenty warriors with poison-tipped arrows while he stood out in the open, unarmed, as bait. Russell eventually admitted to fabricating the story, basing it on a wide range of Native American lore he had heard.

Russell's fiction became legend because there was a blatant void of information around this monster mural that needed filling. The origin and meaning of the beast are a mystery. All we really know is that there was an ancient painting on a limestone bluff that over the centuries took on its modern form as a massive dragon. The people of Alton refuse to let it die, reincarnating it again and again. And good for them.

Cryptozoology Is
for the Birds

Cryptid witnesses might actually be incidental bird watchers. At least, if you believe the theories of skeptics.

Within a week of the first sighting of Mothman, an associate professor of wildlife biology at West Virginia University named Dr. Robert L. Smith confidently claimed to the *Huntington Herald-Dispatch* that the human-sized gray creature with broad wings and large red eyes was almost certainly a sandhill crane—a tall, gray-feathered bird with a seven-foot wingspan and bright red patches around its eyes. Sandhill cranes aren't native to West Virginia, so they would have been an unaccustomed sight, and one or two of them could have easily stopped off in Point Pleasant while migrating south from Canada and the Great Lakes.

In 1955, the Taylor and Sutton families were besieged in an isolated house in Hopkinsville, Kentucky, by three-foot-tall silvery beings with tall ears and wide-spaced eyes. The creatures would come to be known as the Hopkinsville Goblins. In a 2006 issue of *Skeptical Inquirer*, professional skeptic Joe Nickell accepted their description, but stated that it fits a different creature: great horned owls, which are nocturnal and aggressive, especially if protecting a nest. It would also explain why the creatures seemed to float away when shot at.

And then there are thunderbirds, which both cryptozoologists and skeptics agree are birds. But skeptics ascribe less thunder to them. Condors and vultures already get big (with wingspans from six to ten feet), and skeptics note it's easy to misjudge the size of objects in the sky from the perspective of the ground.

I mean, I guess it's all a matter of perspective. But maybe the National Audubon Society should consider opening a cryptid wing.

– Beast of Busco –

TURTLE POWER

TYPE:	EARLIEST SIGHTING:
Reptilian	1948
LOCATION:	SIZE:
Churubusco, Indiana	6 feet long by 5 feet wide, 500 pounds

The welcome sign for Churubusco, Indiana, features a turtle in a sailor hat and dubs the village TURTLE TOWN, U.S.A. Even if you miss that, you'll still notice pretty quickly that the place is turtle obsessed. The dentist is called Turtle Town Dental. Its logo is a tooth shaped like a turtle. The candy store is called Chocolate Turtle. Its turtle logo also wears a sailor's hat. There's a small turtle statue at the crossroads in the center of town and another, much larger one at the local park. The water tower has a sailor turtle on it. Why are there so many cute turtles all over town? Because of a not-so-cute monster—and an epic monster hunt.

It was the summer of 1948. Charlie Wilson and his son-in-law Ora Blue had been fishing all day on a ten-acre pond called Fulk Lake, located on a farm owned by Wilson's sister and brother-in-law, Helen and Gale Harris. Suddenly, Wilson rushed into the house shouting about the biggest turtle he'd ever seen. The Harrises had only owned the farm for about a year at that point, but they'd never seen such a dinosaur of a turtle on the property. Plus, it was Wilson—nobody ever believed him.

Later that year, Gale Harris and his pastor, Orville Reese, were fixing the barn roof when they glimpsed something big splashing around in the lake. They climbed down the roof and jumped into a boat to see what it was. After rowing around for a bit, Reese saw it on his side of the boat—but Harris disagreed because he saw it on his side of the boat. Turns out, they were both right—as was Wilson. Beneath the rowboat lurked a turtle the size of a dining room table, a massive brute of 500 pounds: the Beast of Busco.

Harris told his friends in town what he had seen, and the story spread at the opposite of turtle speed. A report of this giant turtle sighting was sent out on the wire service, and soon the entire country was clamoring over the monster turtle in Fulk Lake. Thousands of people came to the farm from all over, hoping to catch either the reptile itself or just a peek at it. By this time, it was March 1949 and very cold, with parts of the lake still frozen. But, spurred by the widespread interest, plans were hatched to find and catch the beast, encouraged by the Harrises. They hacked a hole in the ice, set up an air compressor, and dropped a diver down there. They tried a crane. They placed traps. They dredged the lake. They even brought in a 225-pound female sea turtle to lure the Beast out. None of it worked, and in the end the people of Churubusco gave up and turned the sea turtle into turtle soup.

Carnival owners offered rewards, neighboring towns with their own lakes tried to claim the Beast as their own, and hoaxes made it into papers. Theories spread. Some speculated that the atomic bomb that had been dropped four years earlier had dislodged the monster from underground. It was a Godzilla story five years before Godzilla hit the screens; a Gamera story before Gamera was even imagined. Some tried to connect the Beast to Chief Little Turtle, a famous Native American leader of the local Miami people, who died a few miles away at Fort Wayne. Maybe he'd returned, as a not-so-little turtle.

Old timers in Churubusco reminded people that this wasn't the first time a giant turtle had been spotted in Fulk Lake. In 1898, the lake's namesake and original owner of the property, Oscar Fulk himself, saw a giant turtle in the water. According to the story, he even swam up to it and carved his name on its shell. Back then, folks called the turtle Oscar. It surfaced again, long enough to be spotted by the subsequent owners of the property in 1914.

In September 1949, Gale Harris decided to pump the lake dry and find this turtle once and for all. He spent weeks pumping it round the clock, sleeping in his car, waiting for the lowering surface to unveil the island hump of a giant turtle shell. Tourists streamed into town again in anticipation of the big moment. And his plan worked. Sort of. On October 13, Oscar was sighted briefly, but slipped away by some unknown route before he could be caught. Eventually, Harris had to give up on both pumping the lake and his entire quest. He had been ignoring his farm all this time and investing too much money into the hunt. It was over. He sold the farm the next year, and Oscar, the Beast of Busco, was never seen again.

But the turtle-shaped void in Churubusco was immediately felt. The locals missed Oscar, so the next year, in 1950, the first Turtle Days was organized. The festival celebrates the exciting hunt for Oscar. Over the decades the annual event has grown to include a parade with turtle floats, fireworks, and turtle races, and Oscar traveled from that lake into the heart and soul of the town. Now you see him everywhere—in much cuter form.

– Van Meter Visitor –

BRIGHT LIGHTS, BIG MONSTER

TYPE:	EARLIEST SIGHTING:
Aerial	1903
LOCATION:	**SIZE:**
Van Meter, Iowa	8 feet tall

The Van Meter Visitor is one of those rare cryptid sto-ries that doesn't begin with teenagers on a back road outside of town. Instead, it begins with respected businessmen in their offices downtown.

Van Meter is a quiet suburb of Des Moines with a population of about a thousand. In the fall of 1903, it was visited by something strange, something that would eventually come to be known as the Van Meter Visitor, one of the more polite names given to a cryptid. It makes it sound like it was cordially invited, rather than shot at by a small militia of armed townsfolk.

On September 29, at one a.m., Ulysses G. Griffith, the owner of a tools and feed business, finished a long day of farm-to-farm selling. He was headed through town toward his home when he noticed a light atop the Mather & Gregg's building. As he observed it, the light quickly jumped across the street to the roof of another building. Before Griffith could figure out what it was, the light blinked out.

The next sighting occurred almost exactly twenty-four hours later and was much less innocuous. A. C. Alcott, the town

THE MIDWEST

doctor, was sleeping in a room behind his office downtown when he was awakened by a bright light shining through his window. Unsure of what it was, but certain it couldn't be good news, he grabbed his gun and ran outside. It was bad news: outside was an eight-foot-tall beaked humanoid with large leathery wings. The blinding light emanated from a single horn on its head. Alcott immediately shot at it—five times, in fact. Five shots that seemed to do nothing to the beaming pterodactyl. Alcott ran back into his office and locked the doors.

The next night, October 1, found Clarence Dunn, a cashier at the local bank and the future mayor of the town, guarding the bank with a shotgun. He wasn't positive that the glowing winged monster he'd heard about was real but thought it highly possible that these tales of strange lights meant robbers were in the area. At one in the morning, the same time as the two previous sightings, he heard a strange noise outside—like something being strangled. A bright light filled the window. He could barely make out a large form behind all that light, but it was terrifying enough for him to squeeze the trigger, blowing out the window. The light disappeared. Dunn went outside to investigate and found a series of three-toed tracks in the mud.

The night of October 2, O. V. White was sleeping in a room above the furniture and hardware store he owned. A loud scraping noise woke him, so he grabbed his gun and looked outside. A dark creature was perched atop a telephone pole across the street. He fired at it, but the monster was unfazed. It turned its light beam on White, who suddenly smelled a strong odor and blacked out.

White's neighbor Sidney Gregg came outside to see what the gunshot was about. He wished he hadn't. What he saw was a giant monster descending the telephone pole, using its huge beak to lower itself down like a parrot on a wooden dowel. Once it reached the ground, it jumped around on two legs, then crawled on all fours. A train roared into town, startling the monster into flight.

By this time, the people of Van Meter were worried: either prominent citizens were going crazy, or something strange was happening in town. Meanwhile, at a brick and tile factory at the edge of town, the strange nest of this strange bird was discovered. On the grounds was an abandoned coal mine, and for the past few days, factory workers had heard all kinds of commotion coming from the hole. The *Des Moines Daily News* stated that the noise was as if "Satan and a regiment of imps were coming forth for a battle." On Saturday, in the early morning of October 3, a factory manager named J. L. Platt decided to check out Satan and his imps for himself. As Platt stood there in the night, at the edge of a deep darkness, he was rewarded for his vigil. At first there was a light, and then the creature burst from the mine. It wasn't alone: after it came a smaller version, also bearing a lit horn. Both flew into the night, their lights eventually lost in the distance.

Platt rallied the factory workers and some locals. They armed themselves and waited for the beast to return to its lair. Finally, at dawn, both creatures reappeared and were welcomed by a storm of gunfire. The two monsters screeched and released foul odors but seemed unharmed by the hail of bullets. They flew into the mine and disappeared. They were never seen again.

The town postmaster, H. H. Phillips, wrote an article about the monster and got it published in the *Des Moines Daily News*. Other papers across the country picked up the story. However, days later, Phillips's account was rebutted in a pair of unauthored articles appearing in the local papers, one in the *Des Moines Daily News* and the other in the *Des Moines Daily Capital*, based on, in the words of the latter paper, "a number of letters from citizens . . . who feel highly indignant over the matter." The unnamed writers acknowledged the strange lights and sounds in town and even Clarence Dunn blasting a hole through the bank window, but claimed this story of light-horned monsters with leathery wings was invented by Phillips. They disavowed the Van Meter Visitor completely.

Van Meter hasn't grown much in one hundred years. The town is still tiny, and the population still hovers around 1,000. However, that's big enough for a monster festival. In 2013, the people of Van Meter threw their first annual Van Meter Visitor Festival, spurred by the release of the book *The Van Meter Visitor* by Chad Lewis, Noah Voss, and Kevin Lee Nelson. It was this book that finally gave the creature both a spotlight and a name. Since that time, Van Meter has been more welcoming to visitors of all kinds.

– Sinkhole Sam –

A REAL CAN OF WORM

TYPE:	EARLIEST SIGHTING:
Aquatic	1952
LOCATION:	SIZE:
Inman, Kansas	15–30 feet long, 21 inches thick

A reporter for the Newspaper Enterprise Association described it as "Kansas's answer to the Loch Ness Monster." *Kansas* City magazine characterized it as "the greatest monster legend Kansas has ever known." You would also not be wrong to call it an oversized worm in a hole.

Twenty-five percent of the counties in Kansas have sinkholes pocking their surfaces. Sinkholes form when the underlying substrata of a section of land is made of a soft rock like sandstone or limestone. When that substrata dissolves, for instance during a heavy rain, the land becomes unsupported and collapses. Sometimes the resulting hole is small or shallow, and sometimes it's big and deep and catastrophic and can eat people and vehicles and entire buildings. And once, a sinkhole came with a cryptid inside. Its name is Sam: Sinkhole Sam.

Big Sinkhole covers an area of about a hundred acres near Inman, Kansas. It's a sinkhole created when an oil company drilled there in the 1920s. These days, it's filled with water and acts as a shallow lake. The depth of Big Sinkhole changes depending on rainfall, and it can get as deep as fifteen feet. But Sinkhole Sam is no mere lake monster. Sinkhole Sam is a giant worm or possibly a snake—but artists usually err on the side of a giant worm instead of the same old wet reptile.

Whatever it is, this tube-like cryptid was discovered in the summer of 1952 by a pair of unnamed fisherman casting their lines at Big Sinkhole. It was described as about twenty-one inches thick, somewhere between fifteen and thirty feet long, with a flat head. The population of the town was just over 600 at that time, so word quickly got around town and eventually beyond it. The monster caught the attention of a journalist named Ernest Dewey, who decided to write about the encounter. Or, rather, to satirize it.

His piece appeared in the *Salina Journal* in November of that year. In it, Dewey claimed that he investigated the sinkhole with his assistant, a scientist named Dr. Erasmus P. Quattlebaum. Without even needing to get their feet wet, they identified the monster as a foopengerkle. According to Dewey, foopengerkles are subterranean, harmless, vegetarian creatures that are both depressed and extinct. However, Dewey warned that since this foopengerkle did not know that it was supposed to be extinct, it might also not know that it's harmless and vegetarian, so the people of Inman should be wary.

The people of Inman weren't wary. They continued to crowd the shores of the sinkhole hoping to be the early birds. Dewey's tongue-in-cheek article even helped stoke some of that sudden tourism. Hundreds showed up, their cars parked around the sinkhole like it was a drive-in movie theater, all hoping to see a real-life creature feature.

The commotion eventually subsided, but at one point in 1923, during a drought, the water level of Big Sinkhole dropped drastically. That had everybody thinking monster thoughts again, since they hoped it would be easier to see—especially after two witnesses came forward. Teenager Albert Neufeld claimed to have fired twice at Sam with his hunting rifle, hitting it and taking care of the town's foopengerkle problem. However, George Regehr claimed to have seen it after the supposed shooting from a short bridge that crossed the hole at the time. He said that Sinkhole Sam seemed safe and whole.

Since then, there hasn't been so much as a ripple from the giant worm. Maybe it went back to the underground caverns that Dewey claimed were the true home of the beast. Maybe it got washed out during one of the area's floods, the same way it might have gotten washed in. And maybe it moved to a more proper lake. In the 1960s, people from the town of Kingman, about an hour south of Inman, organized a hunting party to chase down a twenty-foot-long creature as big around as a man. It had dragged a calf from a local farm into the Kingman County State Lake.

If that was Sinkhole Sam, the people of Inman might want to start appreciating their monster a little more, or they could lose it to Kingman. But who knows—if they're lucky, they'll see it again the next time a big sinkhole opens up.

– Dogman –

PART POOCH, PART PERSON, ALL PANIC

TYPE:	EARLIEST SIGHTING:
Canine-humanoid	1938
LOCATION:	**SIZE:**
Northern Michigan	7–8 feet tall

"I'm a mog—half man, half dog. I'm my own best friend," says John Candy's Barf in the hilarious 1987 Mel Brooks movie *Spaceballs.* But there's a dark side of that combination, too: the Michigan dogman. In Michigan, unlike in every other state in the union, if you see something tall and dark and furry in the forest, you don't think bigfoot. You think dogman.

Descriptions of the creatures vary, from canine heads atop naked human torsos, to human faces with canine snouts and paws for hands, to fully furred dogs that walk on two legs or four. They have blue or amber eyes. Their howls sound more like human screams than a canine bay. They're tall, topping seven feet. The difference between dogmen and cryptid werewolves like the Beast of Bray Road (see page 207) is slim. But the Beast of Bray Road never got a hit radio song.

In 1938, seventeen-year-old Robert Fortney was hunting and fishing on the banks of the Muskegon River near Paris when he was attacked by a pack of wild dogs. He shot his gun above their heads to scare them away, and it worked. Mostly. After four of them scurried off, the fifth one—a big, black-furred brute with blue eyes—stood up on its back legs and stared down the man with the gun. Fortney told an interviewer in 1987, "It may be that I was just scared, but I swear that dog was smiling at me." It finally loped off.

In 1967, two unnamed friends were fishing from a rowboat in Claybank Lake, off the Manistee River, when they saw something swimming toward them. At first they thought it was a deer; then as it got closer, a man; then finally they realized it was something else altogether—something vaguely human but with a long canine snout and paws. It tried to climb in the boat, but the men hit it with an oar. It let go, and they got out of there like their paddles were twin motors.

These stories and others like them, despite taking place in different years, all came out at about the same time: April Fool's Day, 1987. But they weren't jokes. On that day, a radio DJ in Traverse City named Steve Cook released a song he wrote and performed called "The Legend" that *was* supposed to be a joke. It was a spooky spoken-word piece, with shades of Johnny Cash, that listed a series of encounters in Michigan with something called a dogman. These encounters occurred every ten years, on years that ended with a seven, like 1987. In 1887, a crew of loggers gets scared by a dog that stands up. In 1957, a clergyman finds claw marks on the church door higher than any regular dog could have reached. In 1967, a group of hippies get spooked by a dog face smiling at them through their van window.

Cook invented both the dogman and every single one of the vague, bloodless encounters in his song, but when it was released, his radio station was inundated with callers who had encountered the exact creature Cook had described in his song, including the tellers of the Fortney story and the Claybank Lake story. Cook had inadvertently given form and name to an old nightmare, galvanizing all the spooky encounters in the woods of Michigan under the heading of dogman, the same way everything gets lumped under the Jersey Devil in New Jersey.

But then the physical evidence began to pile up. Later that same year, in the tiny village of Luther, a remote cabin got trashed by an animal. Deputy Jeff Chamberlain and another officer responded, assuming before they arrived that it had been a bear. But then they saw the paw prints and bite marks and claw scrapes characteristic of a dog. And some of those bite marks and claw scrapes were on a window frame seven feet off the ground. Immediately, the recently introduced dogman became a prime suspect. Cook even worked the Luther incident into a later version of his song.

In 2007, what would come to be called the Gable Film was anonymously released. It was a three-and-a-half-minute blurry video purportedly found at an estate sale that looked like it was filmed in the 1970s on 8mm. It had no sound but depicted various clips of a family doing normal snowy Michigan activities: riding a snowmobile, chopping wood, walking a dog, working on a truck. Then the video turns menacing, as footage of a forest slowly reveals a dark, furry creature. It spots the cameraperson and moves toward them. The camera operator seems to panic and run. The last frame of the video is a flash of teeth and the view from a camera on its side.

Eventually, the found film was found to be a hoax. The filmmaker, a local named Mike Agrusa, was inspired by his memories of the mass hysteria that Cook's original song had caused, saying in a 2010 episode of the show *MonsterQuest* that it "made the summer of '87 fun." Since 2007 was a "7" year, he made the film and then approached Cook to see if he was up for continuing the legend of the Michigan dogman. Steve was. And the summer of 2007 was a lot of fun too, until they finally revealed the video to be a good-natured prank.

Even though the story of the Michigan dogman is a tangle of hoaxes and dredged-up stories, the stories keep coming: in documentary shows like *MonsterQuest* and *Monsters and Mysteries in America*, in movies like 2012's *Dogman*, and in stories told around campfires in the Northwoods of the state. However, despite Michigan and dogman going together in cryptid circles like Kentucky and goblin, the state hasn't quite caught on to their cryptid treasure. The closest they've gotten is a youth baseball team called the Northern Michigan Dogmen out of Boyne (its mascot is a werewolf-like creature in a red shirt and white shorts), but they have nothing to permanently proclaim Michigan as Home of the Dogman. Maybe they're just waiting for 2027.

—Nain Rouge—

THE DEVIL IN DETROIT

TYPE:	EARLIEST SIGHTING:
Humanoid	1707
LOCATION:	**NOTABLE FEATURE:**
Detroit, Michigan	Red face

I'm not saying that Detroit is a hellhole, but one day a year, its streets fill with thousands of red-faced, horned devils. It's quite the sight.

Often cryptids seem to be the domain of the rural. They are written off as the products of small, isolated towns full of bored, credulous residents who conjure snallygasters from the shadows: bumpkins seeing bigfoot, hicks witnessing hodags. But that's not entirely true. Take the Nain Rouge, a devil that has inhabited the cynical urban landscape of Detroit, Michigan, for over three hundred years.

Nain rouge is a French term that means "red dwarf." Like Louisiana's Rougarou (see page 119), this creature is in part an import from French settlers, who brought with them stories of small, household hobgoblins called lutins. The origin story of the Nain Rouge is recorded in 1884's *Legends of Le Détroit* by local folklorist Marie Caroline Watson Hamlin. She writes that in 1707, six years after French explorer Antoine Laumet de La Mothe Cadillac founded Detroit, he encountered the Nain Rouge, which she describes as an "uncouth figure of a dwarf, very red in the face, with a bright glistening eye" and a "grinning mouth displaying sharp, pointed teeth." Cadillac, despite having been warned of this moment years before by a fortune teller, struck the being with a cane and shouted, "Get out of my way, you red imp!" This act of cruelty doomed Cadillac to a downward spiral that included being exiled to Louisiana, kicked out of the New World, and imprisoned at the Bastille in Paris. Hamlin lists other tragedies precipitated by sightings of the Nain Rouge, including lost battles and city fires.

Author Charles M. Skinner lists a dozen more tragedies caused by the Nain Rouge in his 1896 book *Myths and Legends of Our Own Land*, including the murder of a friar by a Native American who "couldn't endure the tolling of a mass bell" and the destruction of a mill by lightning. He called the Nain Rouge the most "dreaded" of all creatures by the settlers of Detroit.

In more recent times, the Nain Rouge has been spotted before the 12th Street Riot of 1967 and before a 1976 snowstorm that hamstrung the city, as well as various other tragedies and misfortunes. And Detroit has had a lot of tragedies and misfortunes; its infamous economic decay has kept the Red Dwarf busy. In an effort to banish the Nain Rouge and end its reign of terror—at least temporarily—the residents of Detroit banded together with a plan. In 2010, the Marche Du Nain Rouge was organized for the first time, and the people of Detroit proved that it's never too late to celebrate (or berate) your local monster.

The Marche Du Nain Rouge is a cryptid parade with a twist. People attend not to celebrate the creature, but to banish the Nain Rouge from the city for another year. Many dress up in costumes (as anything, really, but the predominant costume is the red devil itself). The costumes help prevent the Nain Rouge from identifying and seeking revenge on the people whose boot prints bruise its arse as they kick it out of town. Some years the Nain Rouge is even burned in effigy.

Each year, a person is selected to officially play the part of the Nain Rouge, and they are responsible for haranguing the parade and all its attendees. In 2016, the *Detroit Metro Times* reported the Nain Rouge impersonator yelling, "I am the legendary Nain Rouge of Detroit, the harbinger of doom, the living embodiment of everything that holds Detroit back, the red prince of persecution, Cadillac's folly, the annihilator of hope!"

But there has been a backlash against the parade by those who feel that the Nain Rouge is misunderstood. To his supporters, the Nain Rouge isn't a curse that brings about Detroit's woes, but rather provides a warning to help the city avoid them. These people protest the parade with tongue-in-cheek signs that say, B NICE 2 NAIN and STOP NAIN SHAME!

If the other chapters of this book are any evidence, those protestors are probably right. Even those who want to banish the Nain Rouge would admit that the parade generates good times, community spirit, and publicity and tourism for the city. Over time, the parade could evolve to celebrate the Red Dwarf rather than evict it. Maybe one day the Nain Rouge will get a statue alongside the city's founder in Hart Plaza, and the Motor City will be better known as "Home of the Nain Rouge."

–Ozark Howler –

CRYPTID WITH A CREEPY CATERWAUL

TYPE:	EARLIEST SIGHTING:
Feline	1810
LOCATION:	**SIZE:**
Ozark Mountains, Missouri	4–5 feet long

In 1810, famous frontiersman and folk hero Daniel Boone was hunting near the Platt River outside of Cuba, Missouri. He was in his mid-seventies, so not as spry as he used to be. Of course, not-as-spry for Boone was still pretty legendary, so when he saw a big, black, horned cat like nothing he'd ever seen in his long life walking through the forest, he calmly lifted his gun and shot at it, no problem. He didn't kill it, just wounded it and scared it away. Of course, if Daniel Boone is in the tale, it's almost certainly a tall one, even setting aside the presence of a monster cat.

The Ozark Howler is usually described as a muscular, broad-shouldered cat about four or five feet in length with a thick, shaggy covering of black hair. Bear-like, really. What's not bear-like is the pair of horns jutting from the top of its head. A giant black cat with horns: that's back-of-a-leather-motorcycle-jacket cool.

As its name would suggest, the beast prowls throughout the wooded flanks of the Ozark Mountains and emits extremely

terrifying howls through its fangy mouth. The sound is typi-
cally described as a mix between a wolf howl and an elk bugle.
That might not sound so terribly terrifying at first blush. However, a quick YouTube search of an elk bugling reveals that it's
an absolutely soul-freezing sound, high-pitched and tortured,
unforgettable, and not at all befitting the majestic elk. It would
raise the goosebumps and neck hair of anybody who heard it,
whether alone at night or at a well-attended birthday party in
the middle of the day.

Most of the Ozark Howler tall tale is of recent vintage—as
in early-internet recent. A big tell that the Ozark Howler is fiction through and through is that it has no landmark sightings,
no period of time when Ozarkians chased and were chased, not
even during the glory days of cryptid sightings in the mid-twentieth century. The few stories that do exist are auditory: someone heard something strange in the forest at night. The only
encounter that gets told is that Daniel Boone folktale—which
also doesn't seem to predate the internet—although another
bit of apocrypha is that Teddy Roosevelt started the entire
National Park Service to protect the territory of this beast.

The real story of the Ozark Howler is that it was a hoax perpetrated on the cryptozoology community at large back in
1998. The pioneering troll would submit sightings to cryptozoology websites, email prominent cryptozoologists, and even
create websites dedicated to the Ozark Howler. In a 2006 Cryp-
tomundo post by Loren Coleman, cryptozoologist and founder
of the International Cryptozoology Museum (see page 38), he
tells how he tracked down the original fraudster whose name
he withheld in exchange for the truth. The person wanted to
show how easy it was to invent a cryptid out of thin air and fool
credulous cryptid lovers. And he proved his point. People still

talk about the Ozark Howler today. I'm talking about the Ozark Howler right now.

So why include the Ozark Howler in this volume? I could say as a cautionary tale of how easy it is to get punked as a cryptid fan. It's practically effortless for any would-be prankster to introduce phantom monsters into a field of borderline-phantom monsters. All you need to do is set up an automated stream of social media posts across scores of puppet accounts, post a few Wix sites, and contribute to a few cryptid wikis. The blind hunger of the twenty-four-hour news cycle across thousands of clamoring outlets is indiscriminate and easy to take advantage of. But the real reason is that I just needed a non-bigfoot cryptid from Missouri to write about (sorry, Momo), and there aren't really any others. It's hard to be a cryptid in the Show Me State. Plus, hoax cryptids are just as fun as the other kind—whatever you believe.

– Walgren Lake Monster –

A GATOR-RHINO WITH
AN IDENTITY PROBLEM

TYPE:	EARLIEST SIGHTING:
Aquatic	1921
LOCATION:	SIZE:
Hay Springs, Nebraska	40 feet long

Here's a twist. How about a lake monster story where it's the lake that doesn't exist? That's what happened in Nebraska when Alkali Lake was renamed Walgren Lake, turning the Alkali Lake Monster into the Walgren Lake Monster— Alky into Wally.

In a place as flat and featureless as the Cornhusker State, it's difficult for a cryptid to hide—unless it's underwater, which is how the Walgren Lake Monster stays out of view. Eyewitness descriptions peg the Alkali ... I mean, the Walgren Lake Monster as a gigantic, stout, alligator-like reptile with a horn set between its eyes and nose. It's anywhere from forty to hundreds of feet long. Wally is not your average sea serpent.

Lake Walgren is located five miles south of the town of Hay Springs in the northwest corner of the state and covers a scant fifty acres. On July 29, 1921, the *Hay Springs News* announced that a mysterious creature had been glimpsed by multiple witness on multiple occasions in then-Lake Alkali, an "octopus or something," maybe eight feet long with a head "the size of a washtub." On September 16, 1921, the same paper discussed further sightings in the months since, still unable to satisfactorily describe the creature. It noted that the thing "seems to be growing larger each time [it's seen]." The title of the report read: IF IT ISN'T A WHALE, IT'S A WHALER OF AN ANIMAL.

Somebody finally got a good view of the creature a month later. In October 1922, three men named J. A. Johnson, Frank Johnson, and John Osborne were hunting for birds on the edge of Lake Alkali. The trio were up early prowling the shore when they saw something in the shallows twenty yards away. It was forty feet long and standing six feet out of the water. It emitted an unpleasant odor. The beast hissed when it saw the men and dived into the deeper water. They saw it briefly in the distance, roiling the surface with its thrashing and slapping the water with a massive tail. In July 1923, J. A. Johnson wrote to the local paper to defend recent eyewitness reports of the creature by defiantly recounting his own close encounter.

In the same month that J. A. Johnson was lobbying for the reality of the creature in the paper, Nebraska residents George Locke, Bob Cook, and two unnamed men from Texas got their car stuck in the mud on the shore of the lake. They spent hours trying to free it, but eventually gave up and decided to just sleep out the night in the car. At two in the morning, they were startled awake by a commotion in the water. According to the *Minden Courier* of Minden, Nebraska, the men saw the massive head and horn of the beast rear up as "high as a giraffe" as it approached the car, which was quickly enveloped by the fog from its nostrils. They escaped and ran two miles until they found a farmhouse to hide in.

The frenzy had elevated to a point where action was demanded by the people of Hay Springs. They discussed purchasing a whaling gun and harpoon. They made plans to dredge the lake, plans which were stymied when the owners of the land demanded $4,000 to lease it for the purpose. International newspapers picked up the story, taking that small corner of Nebraska all the way to London and Paris.

But it wasn't all "we've got to do something about this monster." Many had fun with the creature. Local businesses used it to catch the eye of potential customers, one even displaying a small, preserved mud puppy in its window as a son of the monster. Floats of the creature were included in at least two parades in the state. A "Sea Monster Boat Race" was organized at the lake by the local American Legion.

The Walgren Lake monster ruled the 1920s, and then sightings of it fizzled out after that decade. But it wasn't entirely forgotten. During the centennial of Hay Springs in 1985, they built a replica monster and floated it on the lake, printed T-shirts and buttons, and put it on the welcome sign.

Some say the reason the Walgren Lake Monster disappeared was because it was a hoax perpetrated by businessman John G. Maher, who had a history of pranking the populace. Some say that it disappeared because it was actually a different creature. In 1931, a beaver the size of a car hood was caught by a local trapper, and some considered that to be mystery solved. But in Cryptid Towns, monsters never disappear for long.

– Thunderbird –

BIG, BADASS BIRDS

TYPE:	EARLIEST SIGHTING:
Aerial	Prehistory
LOCATION:	**SIZE:**
North Dakota	Wingspan up to 70 feet

The name bigfoot sounds like an insult, dogman like a junior high nickname that sticks with you through college, and don't get me started on woodbooger. But there's one cryptid with a name so badass it's been folded into pop culture to dub other badassery with. It's the name of a famous United States Air Force jet squadron, a British superhero show from the 1960s, and an iconic sports car from Ford. I'm talking thunderbirds.

Thunderbirds are essentially big birds—big, terrifying birds. According to George M. Eberhart's seminal *Mysterious Creatures: A Guide to Cryptozoology*, the wingspan of a thunderbird can be as long as seventy feet. For comparison, the largest bird in North America, the California condor, has a wingspan of ten feet. The largest bird in the world, the wandering albatross, has a wingspan of twelve feet. You have to go to prehistoric times to find a larger bird: some teratorns had wingspans of twenty feet. Thunderbirds are bigger than some planes.

As such, it's a surprise that they're so hard to spot—especially since thunderbirds are said to darken the sky of every state. They are a continent-wide phenomenon, springing first from the myths and beliefs of numerous native tribes, which inscribe images of them into rock and carve them into totem poles. In the lore of the Comanche, Chippewa, and Mandan, among many others, the thunderbird was the source of storms. Its eyes cracked lightning and its wings beat thunder. It was considered benevolent to humankind, but that didn't make it gentle—it had fierce dust-ups with everything from giant snakes to killer whales.

Thunderbirds are often described as vulture- or condor-like, with dark feathers, a light head, and sometimes a collar of white feathers around its neck. Sometimes, the birds do more than flap around mysteriously; they abduct—usually small animals like calves or dogs, but sometimes children. The most infamous thunderbird abduction (or attempted abduction) of modern times involves a child in Lawndale, Illinois.

On July 25, 1977, ten-year-old Marlon Lowe was playing in his backyard at about eight p.m. His mother, Ruth, was in the kitchen cleaning up when she heard her son scream. She ran outside and saw two giant birds with wingspans of nine or ten feet attacking him, pecking at his head and shoulders until one lifted the fifty-six-pound boy thirty-five feet off the ground. Eventually, both birds gave up on their human prey and disappeared. The incident was seized on by cryptozoologists as being a thunderbird attack. Interestingly enough, Lawndale is only two hours north of Alton, Illinois, home to the Piasa Bird (see page 154). But Illinois isn't celebrating its near-child abduction by giant birds from the sky. That leaves room for another state to claim the thunderbird as its home cryptid: North Dakota.

North Dakota has a talon up on claiming the thunderbird through its rich Native American art, both ancient and new. In the northwest corner of the state, at the borders of Montana and Saskatchewan, is the Writing Rocks State Historic Site. Beneath a simple awning and protected by a rebar barrier is a humble pair of small granite boulders, each about four feet wide, bearing petroglyphs of thunderbirds thought to be anywhere from three hundred years old to over a thousand years old.

Meanwhile, a four-hour drive southeast to the state capital of Bismarck, a modern Native American art installation is keeping the thunderbird alive. In Keelboat Park on the Missouri River is a twenty-foot-tall, ten-foot-diameter, storm-gray statue of four life-sized thunderbird heads. Created by seven students from the United Tribes Technical College in town, these fierce-looking creatures glare atop storm clouds, their claws lifted, lightning in their eyes, beaks majestically crooked, ready to take on any orca or giant snake. Around them, placards tell Native American tales of the thunderbird from different regions of the country, as well as more settler-style cryptid tales like the Lawndale Incident.

Those two bookends from uncounted years in the past to modern day, plus the neverending sky of North Dakota, make it a perfect thunderbird state.

– Dahl Bigfoot –

SASQUATCH VS. THE PRESIDENTS

TYPE:	**CREATED:**
Sculptural	2020
LOCATION:	**SIZE:**
Keystone, South Dakota	22.8 feet tall

South Dakota is not home to a famous bigfoot sighting, but if you go there, you can see one of the biggest bigfoot on the planet.

Let's start with South Dakota's bigfoot history. Sure, the state has its share of bigfoot sightings—all states have their share of bigfoot sightings, even ones as flat and relatively forestless as South Dakota. But the Bigfoot Field Research Organization records only nineteen sightings in the state, making it tied for the eighth lowest number of sightings out of all fifty states. The closest it has to a meaningful bigfoot encounter within its borders is Taku-He, a bigfoot spotted in the McLaughlin-Little Eagle area in the 1970s . . . a bigfoot that wore a coat and top hat. I know you want more detail around that story, but there isn't any. It was just a dapper bigfoot.

Basically, South Dakota was relatively barren of bigfoot, or any cryptids for that matter, until COVID-19 hit the scene. In the autumn of 2020, with the travel and tourism industries devastated, two South Dakota chainsaw artists, brothers Jarrett and Jordan Dahl, had an idea. What could possibly tempt tourists to brave a pandemic that had shut down much of the world, just to visit their chainsaw art shop? The answer was the world's largest chainsaw-carved bigfoot. Obviously. His name is Billie.

Billie is 22.8 feet tall. By comparison, the redwood bigfoot statue at the Willow Creek-China Flats Museum in California is 25 feet tall. The cement statue at the North Fork Survivors Gift Shop in Toutle, Washington, is 28 feet tall. The two-dimensional bigfoot sign at the Gasquatch gas station in Idabel, Oklahoma, is 30 feet tall. But Billie is still bigger than all of those bigfoot. Height isn't everything.

Billie's 22.8 feet is measured from the ground to the crown of his head, and since he is seated, that measurement spans from big butt to big head. But that's only about half of the statue. He languidly sits, one knee bent, the other leg stuck out so that his eight-foot-tall left foot (emblazoned with DAHLS CHAINSAW ART) is extended for photo ops. In his right hand is a tree-trunk-sized flagpole from which flies an American flag. His index finger points off into the distance, and his other arm rests behind him, supporting his enormous weight (Jarret estimates about 30,000 pounds). The Dahl brothers created the gargantuan cryptid from ponderosa pine, cedar, and cottonwood, layering chunks of wood like shingles all over the frame of his body, giving him a furry texture. It took them and a crew eight days to build this *Harry and the Hendersons*–inspired brute, which is more King Kong than bigfoot in terms of scale.

Billie is unceremoniously placed at the edge of the parking lot of Dahl's Chainsaw Art in Keystone, surrounded by a clutter of chainsaw art and tents. It's totally doing its job (there are reports of people driving backward on Route 16A to get a closer look), but the glorious monster deserves a more majestic setting, maybe in the clearing of a woodland somewhere deep in those Black Hills or even the courtyard of a skyscraper.

Although Billie did get his due with a ceremony. When the sculpture was finished, the town of Keystone threw a Bigfoot Bash to welcome their newest tourist attraction and officially measure it for the record books. The town also promised more Bigfoot Bashes to come.

Keystone is primarily known for a different carving, of course: four giant president heads incised into a mountain. Mount Rushmore is only five minutes away from the Dahl bigfoot. As a result, the town has two must-see sculptures, although which one is more must-see is a good question. For the record, I skipped the presidents.

−Loveland Frogman −

HARRY POTTER FROM THE BLACK LAGOON

TYPE:	EARLIEST SIGHTING:
Amphibian-humanoid	1955
LOCATION:	SIZE:
Loveland, Ohio	3–4 feet tall

With the Loveland Frogman, we have a rare cryptid encounter where the police get involved in the story immediately, not as a response to wild late-night claims of terrified teenagers, but as the first witnesses themselves. At one a.m. on March 3, 1972, a police officer in Loveland, Ohio, named Ray Shockey spotted a strange creature in his headlights on Riverside Drive. It was three to four feet tall, with leathery skin and an amphibious head with large eyes, and it was walking on two legs across the street. It leaped a guardrail on the far side of the road and disappeared. It was the kind of encounter that maybe you don't log officially—you chalk it up to the late-night hours and the pressures of the job. Except that there was a precedent for amphibious humanoids in Loveland, an urban legend that had been passed around town for years. It seemed that one of the Loveland Frogmen was back.

The original story goes that in 1955, an unnamed businessman was headed through Loveland late one night. Whether he was a local or just passing through is also unknown. He saw a clump of three or four forms on the side of the road along the

Little Miami River, a tributary of the Ohio River that bisects the town and is spanned by many bridges. He stopped the car in shock when he realized that the forms weren't people. They were three- to four-foot-tall bipedal creatures with grayish, leathery skin, webbed feet and hands, and amphibious faces. In other words, frog people. I imagine them sort of like Gollum in the Rankin/Bass animated version of *The Hobbit*.

Nobody knows the origin of the urban legend, but it does have a few variations, depending on whether the teller wants to file the story under cryptid lore or extraterrestrial lore. In the former, the mere existence of these humanoid frogs scares the businessman back into his car. In the latter, as the businessman stares, the creatures seem to be whispering to each other, and then one of them holds up a wand that starts sparking and shooting light, Harry Potter–style. And that's what startles the businessman into exiting the story stage right.

Two weeks after Officer Shockey's apparent encounter with a decades-old urban legend, he got backup from one of his colleagues. Officer Mark Matthews was driving the same area of Loveland late at night on St. Patrick's Day when he saw a crumpled form on the road. Thinking it was a dead animal, he pulled over and exited his vehicle to scrape its carcass off the asphalt before it caused an accident. When he got closer, he discovered that it was a reptile of some sort, about three to four feet long. It reminded him of the description that Shockey had given. That description was confirmed when the creature jumped up on two legs and Froggered across the road to the guardrail. Matthews pulled out his gun and shot at the creature, but it jumped the metal barrier and got away. And that's probably where the story would end, if the Pokémon Go craze hadn't hit us in the mid-2010s.

On August 3, 2016 (a month after the augmented reality game was released), a young man named Sam Jacobs was playing one night with his girlfriend at the edge of Lake Isabella, which parallels the Little Miami River. As they searched for Pokémon, they saw something rise from the lake and walk through the shallow water on two legs. It was about four feet tall with glowing eyes. Since Jacobs had his phone on hand to capture virtual monsters, he used it to take photos and video of this real-life monster. The grainy pics and dark footage show a lumpy form with giant, glowing eyes. In an interview with a local NBC affiliate, Jacobs called it a "frogman or just a giant frog."

In a surprise twist, this new chapter of the Loveland frogman saga helped bring closure to an old chapter. The stories and photos that ran in the press about Jacobs's sighting often referenced the 1972 encounters by the police force. Officer Mark Matthews, who was now retired in Florida, read the story and came forward to set the record straight. He said that most of his story was true, except for how it ended. He had actually shot the creature, which he said was already half dead from the cold. When he retrieved the corpse, he found it to be a large iguana with its tail missing. He showed its body to Shockey, who agreed that it was what he had seen, relieved that he wouldn't be going down in the books as the crazy Loveland Frogman cop (oops). Matthews believed the creature to be an escaped pet that had kept warm by sticking around the outlet pipes from the nearby Totes boot factory. According to Matthews, he had told the whole story to an author putting together a book of Ohio legends, but the author had omitted the big reveal.

But despite Matthews's myth-busting, the frogmen still thrive in the lore of Loveland. The town doesn't have a museum or a statue dedicated to them yet, nor an annual festival in their honor. But you do see them pop up here and there. The Loveland Frogman race is an annual amphibious triathlon in Loveland. You see them on T-shirts. They were even the subject of a musical in nearby Cincinnati. The Loveland frogmen are a mere historical plaque by the river away from being an official mascot for the town.

–Peninsula Python –

SHINDIG FOR A SNAKE

TYPE:	EARLIEST SIGHTING:
Reptilian	1944
LOCATION:	**SIZE:**
Peninsula, Ohio	15–18 feet long

Pythons aren't cryptids. They're, I don't know, pythons.
You can get one at your local pet store. But if you find them in
the wrong place, outside their natural habitat, and if they are
terrifying the populace, or if there's a hint that they might be
part of an undiscovered thriving population, they become a
subset of cryptid hilariously called OOPS, for out-of-place species. One of the most celebrated examples of an OOPS in the US
is the Peninsula Python of Ohio.

Peninsula is a small canal town straddling the Cuyahoga
River between Cleveland and Akron. It is not, in fact, a peninsula, but named such due to the way the river coils around the
center of town, making it look like a peninsular protrusion.
But in the summer of 1944, more than the Cuyahoga snaked
through the town. A massive python both terrorized and
amused Peninsula for months.

On June 8, farmer Clarence Mitchell became its first witness when he saw it cutting a trail through his cornfield. It was
no mere corn snake, though: he estimated the reptile at somewhere between fifteen and eighteen feet long. On June 10, Paul

and John Szalay found similarly sinuous tracks in their fields, the width of a tire track. On June 12, things escalated beyond mere trespassing when Mrs. Roy Vaughn saw the python squeezing through a fence, a lump in its body making the process laborious. She realized later she was missing a chicken.

Newspapers picked up the story. Both the Cleveland and Columbus zoos responded with offers of help. Scores of hunters beat the bushes looking for this OOPS serpent (although a big emphasis was put on not killing the snake, and guns were mostly left home). Sometimes the posses found tracks, sometimes false alarms, but never the serpent itself. Still, in the words of a reporter from the *Akron Beacon Journal* who joined one of the hunts, "that snake is no joke to the Peninsula folks."

On June 27, Pauline Hopko noticed that her cows were agitated. Soon she joined them in their agitation as the giant snake slunk from the branches of a nearby tree. That same day it was also sighted by a group of local boys. On June 29, Mrs. Ralph Griffin saw it in her yard, lifting its head six feet into the air. Ernest Raymond saw a stump in his field that hadn't been there before. When it moved, he realized it was the coiled python.

Authorities always seemed to arrive too late when these encounters were reported. And they continued to arrive too late, as sightings didn't abate until summer ended. The town, unable to catch the thing, decided to wait it out, knowing a python couldn't survive an Ohio winter. When it turned cold, they looked for a stiff coil of reptile flesh against the white snow—but it never turned up, belly up or otherwise.

Was it a case of mass hysteria? Did it find a way to survive the winter? Did it migrate south? Nobody knows, nor do they know where it came from. An urban legend sprouted about a crashed circus train (the circus often gets blamed for cryptid sightings).

Another theory held that the python was a mutant from the Krejci Dump, which opened four years earlier a few miles north of town. Nobody knew it then, but four decades later, the discovery that its owners were accepting illicit chemical waste would cause the land to be classified as a Superfund site. Most thought the python might be an escaped pet, although nobody claimed it.

Large OOPS snakes have popped up in other towns. In 2016 in Westbrook, Maine, a nine-foot-long anaconda was spotted sporadically throughout the summer, including swimming in the Presumpscot River with a beaver in its mouth. That snake also disappeared, but it did leave behind a shed skin, which is now enshrined at the International Cryptozoology Museum in Portland (page 38).

But nowhere else honors their OOPS like Peninsula. For decades, they have celebrated Peninsula Python Day, on which residents festoon their homes and places of business with fake snakes like some people hang lights at Christmas. A parade snakes through town, often with a giant float of the creature in the lead. Peninsulans eat foot-long python-dogs, bring in real pythons, and in general just throw a real python party.

I missed Python Day by a month, and when I drove through the town I saw no fake snakes entwined around porches or park trees. The only telltale sign was at the local library. On its exterior wall is a mural of Peninsula, the Cuyahoga River twisting so much like a giant snake that I at first thought it was the python itself. My disappointment was soon assuaged, though, as inside the library I found a towering painting of the snake that seemed as tall as the original snake was long. Whether the Peninsula Python is a mere tall tale or not, few actual people make a mark on their towns like it has.

OOPS, I Cryptid Again

It is the greatest acronym in cryptozoology: OOPS. It stands for out-of-place species. The term applies to scientifically proven animal populations that are reportedly thriving in the wild where those animals aren't supposed to—or even physically shouldn't be able to.

An example is the phantom kangaroo. Kangaroos are found natively only in Australia, but there have been reports of them in the wild across the United States, especially in the Midwest. OOPS animals can also include OOTS, a rarely used acronym for out-of-time species, which are animals reported in areas where they have gone extinct. An example is sightings of giant felids—cougars, jaguars, even lions—in areas where they don't exist anymore. Cougars used to roam New England as late as the 1800s. Lions roamed North America 11,000 years ago. When sighted in those places, these felids are also known as alien big cats, or ABCs, the second greatest acronym in cryptozoology.

While it's physically possible for kangaroos and lions to live in certain areas of the United States (and escaped zoo animals and pets are often blamed for these sightings), other types of OOPS are more exotic. For instance, an urban legend has long placed alligators in the cold, contaminated sewers of Manhattan. The Oklahoma Octopus (page 145) is supposed to live in freshwater lakes in the state, even though no species of octopus currently known can survive in fresh water. The Peninsula Python of Ohio could never tolerate the harsh winters of that Great Lake town, and yet Peninsula celebrates the long reptile every year.

The image is a great one though—a deity up there making animals on whatever day of creation, placing them carefully in their custom-designed environments, and then accidentally dropping a bunch of kangaroos on the wrong continent. "Oops," says the Almighty.

-Underwater Panther -

SUBURBAN MOUND MONSTER

TYPE:	EARLIEST SIGHTING:
Aquatic	Prehistory
LOCATION:	**NOTABLE FEATURE:**
Granville, Ohio	Yellow fur or scales; horns

I have never seen a creepier neighborhood than Bryn Du Drive in Granville, Ohio. The houses on this cul-de-sac are nice, the lawns tended—relatively unremarkable, when focused on individually. But collectively, they surround a 1,000-year-old mound shaped like a creature not recognized by modern zoology—an evil creature, in fact: the underwater panther. The houses encircling it look like they were built in that careful arrangement by a worshipful cult waiting for the monster to arise.

Effigy mounds are ancient Native American ceremonial mounds that were thought to be built primarily between 350 and 1300. They can be shaped like animals, people, or symbols. There are thousands of them scattered throughout the Midwest, but Ohio claims two of the biggest and scaliest ones: the Alligator Effigy Mound and the Great Serpent Mound.

The Great Serpent Mound in Peebles is the largest effigy mound in the country. Its sinuous curves extend 1,348 feet in the shape of a snake swallowing an egg-shaped object. To see it, you pay admittance, loiter inside a small museum, and then walk around the mound before ascending a tower to see the snake in all its glory. Something akin to that experience is what I expected with the Alligator Mound, which is 120 miles away from the Great Serpent Mound and just outside of Columbus. So I was surprised when I pulled down Bryn Du Drive and saw no interpretive museum, no tower. It's just a private neighborhood with a grassy hump in the middle. A lonely historical placard is the only indication that atop that hill is a 200-foot-long effigy mound.

The setting isn't the only surprise with Alligator Mound. Despite its name, it's not shaped like an alligator. It's impossible to see the full shape of the mound from ground level. If you ascend the hill (and ignore the feeling that window blinds are being parted all around you), you can see areas at the top that are higher and rounded, but that's it. Arial photographs reveal a round head, four splayed legs, and an arcing tail—nothing like an alligator. Researchers believe that when European explorers were first shown the mound by Native Americans, they mistranslated the Native American name for it. The builders of the mound may have described a water monster, which the Europeans assumed to be an alligator. But alligators aren't native to Ohio: the underwater panther is.

The underwater panther is four-legged, covered in short, yellowish fur or scales, has a long tail, and horns on its head. Most ancient and modern depictions of it show a cat-reptile hybrid, and it's a mean one. In the lore of multiple native tribes of the Midwest, it's an enemy of the benevolent thunderbird (see page 182) and it attacks humans, pulling them into the water to drown. Some researchers even believe that the original Piasa Bird mural in Alton, Illinois (see page 154), depicted an underwater panther before modern artists added wings to it.

The underwater panther is also a possible source of Wisconsin's beloved hodag (see page 211).

As with Great Serpent Mound, the exact purpose and builders of the Alligator Mound are unknown, but there are guesses. At one point it was thought that the Hopewell people built it, but these days the prevailing idea is that it is a Fort Ancient culture artifact. Also, it's definitely not a burial mound (easy enough to test) but might have been used for ceremonial or social purposes.

The historical placard at the Alligator Mound does admit in small print that the mound is not shaped like an alligator. It mentions that the mound could represent a possum or a (land) panther. But would a dark cosmic cult build their houses around the rebirth of a mere evil possum? Doubtful.

–Dawson Gnome –

A LOCAL IMP-FESTATION

TYPE:	CREATED:
Sculptural	1989
LOCATION:	**SIZE:**
Dawson, Minnesota	3 feet tall

Maybe you wouldn't find it terribly interesting to see a large cluster of three-foot-tall concrete gnomes in a town park. But what if I told you that those gnomes were once people, that the town had squeezed its residents down into diminutive versions of themselves, added conical hats, and then put them on display? Because that's what Dawson, Minnesota, does.

Gnomes are small, humanoid creatures of European origin, often lumped into the same category as goblins, dwarves, and leprechauns. The name comes from the Latin *genomos*, which means "earth-dweller." They live underground and travel through dirt like we travel through air, guarding treasures of precious metals and gems. At least, that's what gnomes used to be known for. These days, in the US, we mostly know them as pointy-hatted, white-bearded garden decorations, a tradition which originated hundreds of years ago with German craftspeople, who called them Gartenzwerge, and later the English aristocracy, who used the statues as status symbols. That's right—garden gnomes used to be kingly instead of kitschy.

But Dawson—or, as it styles itself, Gnometown, USA—has

a totally unique approach to garden gnomes. Dawson is a small town of 1,400 close to the South Dakota border. Every year since 1989, Dawson has chosen a resident (or multiple residents) of the town—not for a Shirley Jackson–style lottery, but to honor them for their service to the community. And they accomplish that with a very unusual statue: a gnomified version of the honoree. You can tell a Dawson gnome from your garden-variety garden gnome because a Dawson gnome's hat is bent, and there is a heart on its sleeve. Each gnome is unique, by virtue of either its outfit, an item it's holding, or an activity it's engaged in, each detail signifying the person being honored. The gnome of a basketball coach wears a jersey and holds a basketball; the gnome of a music director waves a conductor's wand; the gnome of a doctor wears a white coat and a stethoscope necklace. In Dawson, being depicted as a gnome is the highest honor, and not the insult it would be anywhere else in the country.

The town's infatuation with gnomes can be credited to two sisters. In 1987, the town council was looking for something they could market the town with. Dawson needed a "thing," like the giant ball of twine that the neighboring town of Darwin touted. Residents Alta Roesch and Ruth Solem were discussing the situation on a shopping trip when Roesch, the local librarian, brought up European gnomes, which she had been reading about. "We should be Gnometown, USA," she said. The two women brought the idea to the town council, where it was adopted. Another resident and friend of the sisters, Sharilyn Bates, loved the concept and came up with the idea of honoring citizens with gnome effigies. The three women were instrumental in not just kickstarting the program, but also shepherding it over the years.

The town unveils the gnome of honor at the annual Riverfest

event, which started the year before Dawson become Gnometown, USA. The new gnome is placed in the park on the east side of town off Oak Street. The gnomes are mostly arranged around the WELCOME TO DAWSON sign there. A biography of the gnome-person in fable form is also prepared, which can be read online. When the town first started the tradition, the original gnomes were carved from wood. Those are now on display inside the local library to protect them from the elements. These days, the painted concrete gnomes can take whatever the Minnesota winter throws at them.

Currently, Gnometown contains about forty-five gnomes. In 2020, Riverfest was cancelled due to the COVID-19 pandemic. For the 2021 celebration, Dawson tried something new, focusing on an initiative called Triumph Over the Troll. Instead of gnomifying a resident, they personified the virus itself as an ugly troll named Covidius Putrid Evilson the 19th and added it to the collection to mark how the town came together during that dark time to defeat the creature.

If you ever visit Dawson, make sure you pay your respects to three gnomes in particular. In 2012, Gnometown, USA, added Alta, Ruth, and Sharilyn to its ranks, three women who had a real gnome run of an idea.

«———◆———»

— Wendigo —

FROSTY THE FLESHEATER

TYPE:	EARLIEST SIGHTING:
Humanoid	Prehistory
LOCATION:	**NOTABLE FEATURE:**
Upper Midwest US; Lake Windigo, Wisconsin; Minnesota	Cannibalistic

The legend of the wendigo originated with the Algonquin in what is now Canada and the northern United States. And then settlers ran with it. And then everyone ran from it together.

The wendigo (also windigo, among other spellings) has metamorphosed over the centuries, splitting into three versions of the creature. All of its incarnations are frightening, though, because of what it represents fundamentally. It started out, according to the Ojibwe People's Dictionary, as a "winter cannibal monster," three of the most terrifying words in any language. This wendigo is a giant, soaring anywhere from ten feet tall to higher than the pine trees of the northern forests. It's described as humanlike, but emaciated, with a face blackened by frostbite and missing lips and cheeks because it chewed them off in its hunger for human flesh. Its diet is described succinctly by George M. Eberhart in his book *Mysterious Creatures: A Guide to Cryptozoology*: "Eats people, especially children." The wendigo is a personification of the ice and hunger, cold and death, despondence and desperation that rime the winter

wastelands of North America.

But it's not just a metaphor for the ruthlessness of those climes. It's a human monster, one whose dangerous greed and murderous inclinations can ruin a community in an environment where trust and working together are vital for survival. This version of the wendigo, an extension of the original tale, is the idea that anybody who puts their survival needs above others' and eats human flesh (or is tempted to) can "go wendigo." They are possessed by the spirit of the wendigo, their hearts and spines encased in ice so thick that you can hear it popping and cracking if you put your ear to their chest. The only cures for wendigoism are either to pour hot bear fat down the person's throat to melt that ice—or to kill them.

In December 1897, the *Saint Paul Globe* of Minnesota reported that a Native American woman living in the Berens River Reserve of Manitoba had contracted typhoid fever, the effects of which caused her to act strangely. Her husband thought she was going wendigo, so he grabbed her by the hair and broke her neck. He was arrested for murder. But there are also cases of people going wendigo that are not mistaken diagnoses. The most infamous is the case of Swift Runner.

It was just after the winter of 1878 to 1879 in Alberta. A Cree man named Swift Runner who was known and liked in town returned from his winter camp without his family, behaving strangely. He said that they had died of starvation, even though he looked pretty hale for a man who had survived a winter that killed the other nine members of his family. The North West Mounted Police decided to check in on him. What they found was a camp strewn with human bones—some of them gnawed. Swift Runner confessed to what the academic world calls anthropophagy, and the rest of us call cannibalism.

He said he'd been having strange dreams, and that a spirit told him to eat his family, which included his wife, brother, mother, and six children ("Eats people, especially children"). He'd gone wendigo. It was a harsh winter, but it wasn't an eat-your-family harsh winter. Swift Runner even admitted that he killed and ate one of his sons, the last of his family to die, so that there would be no witnesses to his crimes. Swift Runner was hanged for the ghastly murders in December 1879 at Fort Saskatchewan. The true motivation for his atrocities will never be fully parsed, but for a few decades in the twentieth century, some psychiatrists diagnosed and treated "wendigo psychosis" as a culture-bound syndrome.

In modern times, pop culture has gentled the Wendigo into a winter spirit often depicted as either a humanoid deer with antlers or a ghostly creature with a deer or elk skull for a head—terrifying in its own way if witnessed on a snowy night in the woods. Meanwhile, states adjacent to Canada that also know the mental and physical burden of difficult winters annexed the wendigo to their own lore, most notably Minnesota and its neighbor Wisconsin, the latter of which has made inroads into making the claim official.

Stoughton, Wisconsin, is the home of a restaurant called Wendigo, which features a Cannibal Burger on its menu that's stuffed with tenderloin and bacon. And every October, the town of Manitowac has a Windigo Fest, which is a Halloween celebration with haunted attractions, a spooky parade, live music, and sideshows.

Minnesota hasn't made those kinds of moves to embrace the wendigo, but it does have a strange natural anomaly called Lake Windigo. It's a 199-acre lake in the middle of a star-shaped island in the middle of another lake called Cass Lake. That's right: Lake Windigo is a lake within a lake.

In the late twentieth century, a researcher named Carol Crawford Ryan gathered stories from locals about Lake Windigo, some of which seemed to go back hundreds of years. She heard that a wendigo is supposed to live in the icy waters of that inner lake. Bare footprints and exit holes from some large thing or things are found on the ice when the lake freezes over. She heard that the lake was used as a big kettle by a group of cannibal giants for boiling humans, and that a Native American chief had ventured to the island and never returned.

That makes Windigo Lake a good place for a statue, I think. Or a historical marker. At least a warning sign. Either way, only time will tell which state, Minnesota or Wisconsin, will be the better claimant for one of the scariest creatures in this book.

–Beast of Bray Road–

WEREWOLVES OF WISCONSIN

TYPE:	**EARLIEST SIGHTING:**
Canine-humanoid	1989
LOCATION:	**SIZE:**
Elkhorn, Wisconsin	6–8 feet tall, 150 pounds

Ask any cryptozoologist if they believe in zombies and they'll say, "Nah, that's Halloween stuff." Vampires? "No, those are from a more superstitious time." Resurrected mummies? "Horror movie monsters." What about werewolves? Do werewolves exist? They'll pause at that one, tilt their head, and say, "Sort of."

Bray Road is a pretty straight-shot four-mile road in Walworth County, Wisconsin. It connects the edge of the town of Elkhorn (population 10,000) to Route 11. The road cuts through cornfields and farms. Sporadic copses line its edges. And this unlikely setting is the haunt of humanoid wolves. On December 29, 1991, a county newspaper called the *Week* ran an article with the title TRACKING DOWN 'THE BEAST OF BRAY ROAD,' complete with an illustration of a crouched wolfman holding a dead animal in its hands/front paws. The article caused a sensation.

The journey to that article began with stories whispered among local Elkhorn teenagers, which were overheard by a bus driver, who relayed the rumor to newspaper cartoonist and burgeoning journalist Linda S. Godfrey. Godfrey chased the story down, and when she interviewed the man who ran animal control in the area, he pulled out a folder labeled "werewolf." That's when she knew she had found a story. She wouldn't know until much later that she had found a lifelong obsession.

That folder revealed that for the past few years, people had been seeing werewolves near that simple stretch of Bray Road. In 1989, Lori Endrizzi was driving at 1:30 in the morning when she saw a hump by the side of the road. As she neared, that vague shape revealed itself to be a 150-pound man-shaped thing covered in dark brownish-gray fur. It feasted on the roadkill it was holding in its claws. "I remembered the long claws," she told Godfrey. Endrizzi sped past until it disappeared behind her.

On a foggy Halloween night in 1991, a high school senior named Doris Gipson was driving Bray Road when her car softly thumped. She stopped the car and got out to see if she had hit something when a huge, furry form on two legs came running at her. She jumped back in the car. As she smashed the gas, she heard the scrape of claws on the trunk. She would later show the scratch marks to Godfrey. Another teenager driving through on a foggy night saw a dark form but couldn't make out any details—only its massive claws as it swiped at the vehicle, damaging it.

Those were just a few of the many stories from the previous few years that Godfrey unearthed for her report. When the Beast of Bray Road piece ran in the *Week*, she received even more stories from readers. The creature was generally described as fanged, with red eyes, dark fur, and the head of a wolf (or sometimes the head of a German Shepherd). But what made it a werewolf was that it was bipedal, standing somewhere between six and eight feet tall, with the furred body of a man.

The normally quiet Bray Road quickly became the Las Vegas

strip. Wannabe werewolf hunters wandered nearby farms with flashlights and guns. A highway's worth of cars poured down the scant four miles of road, hoping to catch furred monsters in their headlights. Tour buses lumbered through. A sign went up on Bray Road that said WEREWOLF AREA. A plywood cutout of the beast was placed in a nearby yard. Meanwhile, in Elkhorn, enterprising businesses offered werewolf-shaped cookies and T-shirts and Silver Bullet Specials. Godfrey herself became a celebrity as media from all over the country contacted her to learn more about the monster. Some of those media sources called the monster the "Wisconsin Werewolf" or the "Walworth County Werewolf," but the name that stuck was Godfrey's: the Beast of Bray Road.

Soon after her article was published, Godfrey received a call from a local newspaper editor named Joe Schackelman who told her a story about his father, Mark, that intimated an occult origin to the creature. In 1936, the elder Schackelman was a nightwatchman at the St. Coletta School for Exceptional Children in the adjoining county of Jefferson. One midnight, he was patrolling the grounds when he saw a form at the top of one of the many ancient Native American burial mounds on the property. The creature smelled like dead meat and was digging furiously in the dirt. When his flashlight disturbed the beast, it stood up to reveal itself to be a furry, wolf-faced creature that ran off on two legs. The next midnight, when Shackleman returned to the spot, the creature was atop the same mound, scrabbling in the dirt again. This time the creature stood up and said something before it ran off: "Gadara." Godfrey tied the utterance to the story of the miracle of the Gadarene swine in the biblical Gospels, in which a man from the city of Gadara was possessed by a legion of evil spirts that Jesus cast out and sent into a herd of pigs, which promptly went mad and ran into a lake to their deaths. Adding fuel to the hypothesis that the werewolf was possessed was the fact that one of the priests connected to St. Coletta was an exorcist.

Whether demon possessed or dogman, the Beast frenzy eventually died down. People stopped reporting sightings, local businesses stopped capitalizing on it, and Elkhorn went back to being an idyllic Midwestern town instead of the set of a horror movie. It wasn't the last time werewolves were seen out there, though. Another uptick in beast sightings occurred in 2003 after Godfrey published her book *The Beast of Bray Road: Tailing a Wisconsin Werewolf*. Today, the only sign that Bray Road was once the haunt of werewolves is a six-foot-tall wooden statue in the front yard of one of the homes on the road. But you never know. Maybe one day it'll be rejoined by its living counterparts, and Bray Road will be a werewolf wonderland once again.

– Hodag –

EVERY DAG HAS ITS DAY

TYPE:	**EARLIEST SIGHTING:**
Mammalian	1893
LOCATION:	**NOTABLE FEATURES:**
Rhinelander, Wisconsin	Greenish fur; row of spikes down back and tail

In 2021, the governor of the state of Wisconsin, Tony Evers, proclaimed May 21 as Hodag Day. In his announcement, he said, "No matter where you're from, the hodag is a key part of our culture, identity, and heritage." The hodag is a cryptid.

The hodag is about the size of a black bear, covered in greenish fur, and bristling with bony spikes down its back and tail. The two long tusks in its upper jaw match the pair of horns atop its head and its long claws. In William T. Cox's *Fearsome Creatures of the Lumberwoods*, a tongue-in-cheek collection of lumberjack folklore from 1910, he acknowledges that description but submits a different version of the hodag that he finds more believable. His money is on the hodag being a rhino-sized, shovel-faced creature whose patterned coat inspired lumberjack plaid. But the city of Rhinelander, Wisconsin, in the heart of the Wisconsin Northwoods, chose the thorny version as its mascot. Although mascot is not an adequate term. I don't think I've ever seen a community commit to a monster like Rhinelander does with the hodag. The place puts every bigfoot town to shame.

The story of the hodag might begin with the Native Americans, as some have remarked on the distinct similarity between the horned hodag and ancient depictions of the underwater panther (see page 196). Its story goes back at least as far as the aforementioned lumberjacks, whose stories Cox collected in the early twentieth century. Rhinelander was established in 1882 as a lumber town, with its burly axe wielders working to thin out the nearby Northwoods. For the lumberjacks, the hodag was considered a ghost, the spirit or maybe even the reincarnation of a dead ox that spent its life lugging logs. The beast of burden couldn't quite release its earthly burden and stuck around to haunt the forests and lumber camps.

The person who elevated the hodag in the public imagination was a Rhinelander businessman named Gene Shepard. In 1893, Shepard started showing people photographs he claimed to have taken of the beast (which some say he described as foul-smelling and fire-breathing) after hunting it down with a few partners. The group tried to take it down with rifles and water pistols full of poison, but eventually had to resort to dynamite. In 1896, Shepard took the gag further by claiming to have trapped a hodag in its den with the help of some bear wrestlers by blocking the opening with rocks. He then knocked the hodag unconscious with a sponge soaked in chloroform on the end of a stick. Shepard took the creature on tour to various county fairs. The hodag specimen was actually a wooden puppet covered in black hair that was manipulated in the dim tent via wires.

All that effort really cemented the creature in the history of Rhinelander. Fast forward to today, and it's impossible to avoid the hodag while passing through town. There are statues of it everywhere, themed businesses, gift shops (don't pass up the Ho-Ho-Hodag Christmas sweaters and tree ornaments), local museum exhibits, welcome signs, street pole banners, and historical placards. The hodag is the high school mascot. It has an annual week-long festival in May called Hodag Heritage Days (which was launched as part of the governor's Hodag Day announcement), not to be confused with the Hodag Country Festival (a music event established in 1978). The centerpiece of all that hodaggery is a large statue that sits in front of the Chamber of Commerce. Finally, the town website, explorerhinelander.com, is literally a hodag fan site. You can learn the history of the creature, play hodag video games, and join the fan club. I could barely find any information on the actual town.

In many ways, Rhinelander is the shining example of how I want all towns to celebrate their cryptids. But it's also an opportunity to ask oneself, "Can you take cryptid commemoration too far?" I don't know the answer, but whatever it is, it's definitely in Rhinelander, Wisconsin. Happy Hodag Day!

– Rhinelapus –

LOVECRAFT'S GUMBY

TYPE:	CREATED:
Sculptural	Early 1940s
LOCATION:	**NOTABLE FEATURE:**
Monico, Wisconsin	Three tentacular legs

This is a weird one. So weird that my editor tried to kill it. But you can't kill the Rhinelapus, because it's not so much a cryptid as it is a meta-cryptid. And that's why I love it.

Monico, Wisconsin, has a population of less than 400. It's one of those towns that you have to zoom in extremely close on Google Maps for its name to appear. On the western edge of town, on the side of US 8, under a copse of tall conifers, is a small chain-link enclosure around a pavilion that is barely big enough to contain the monster inside. The large, gangly green beast has white feet with black claws at the end of three tentacular legs. It has a blunt head with beady red eyes and a white horn set just behind its skull. It looks as if H. R. Giger tried his hand at designing a cryptid. It's nightmarish, in other words—like a Lovecraftian god, or a Lovecraftian Gumby. It's one of the more terrifying-looking beasts in this entire collection, in fact. That creature in that little park pavilion is the Rhinelapus. And I mean that literally. It's not a statue of the Rhinelapus—it *is* the Rhinelapus.

Sometime in the early 1940s, a local tavern owner by the

name of Guy Daily found a large, curious-looking pine stump with a set of swollen, twisted tree roots near Monico Creek. It looked like something more than just a stump to him—something interesting—something he thought that other people might like to see. He was inspired to hack the SUV-sized growth out of the ground and haul it back to his establishment, the Lake Venus Tavern in Monico. There, he set it up on the porch as a curiosity. He thought the wooden Rorschach test looked like a combination of a rhinoceros, an elephant, and an octopus, so he dubbed it Rhinelapus. The beast was eventually painted green to help preserve and define it, which is how it got its other name, the Green Monster.

The Rhinelapus loomed in front of the Lake Venus Tavern for sixty years, dominating the entrance while scaring, delighting, confusing, and drawing visitors. Children would climb on it. Tourists would take photos with it. Old postcards and photos of the tavern showed the strange tentacular monster under the roofed porch, even if the captions eerily refused to explain what the heck that thing was. The Rhinelapus even outlived Daily himself.

In 2002, the Rhinelapus became endangered. The latest owner of the restaurant wanted to get rid of it. Maybe they were terrified of it; maybe they didn't quite understand the benefits of being a monster-themed eatery. Whatever the reason, they wanted it gone and mentioned it to a local named Bob Walkowski, saying that if the thing wasn't removed, they would have to chop it into green firewood. Knowing how much history this random growth of wood had seen, Walkowski called up a friend named Robert Briggs, who was the town chairman. Briggs brought an excavator and a dump truck to transport the oddity to its current location, Monico Town Park. I like to imagine that the delivery was as tension-filled as the first scene of *Jurassic Park*. Today, the Rhinelapus still haunts the entrance to the park. In fact, it became an official ward of the town, which is, according to a sign on its enclosure, "responsible for its care and feeding."

Somehow, in all those decades since it was torn from its natural habitat, the creature hasn't accrued any lore beyond its origin story as a tangle of pine wood. Nor has it risen to the level of the beloved hodag (see page 211) in neighboring Rhinelander (just fifteen miles away), although there is a one-sided rivalry between the towns. The joke in Monico is that the Rhinelapus feeds on hodags. But even without any lore or fancy festivals in its honor, the Rhinelapus offers an important lesson: if your town lacks a cryptid, you can simply make your own.

–Mount Horeb Troll–

THE TROLLWAY OR THE HIGHWAY

TYPE:	SIGHTING:
Sculptural	1980s
LOCATION:	**SIZE:**
Mount Horeb, Wisconsin	2–6 feet tall

Trolls are slippery monsters. The term can mean any-thing from an ogre-like giant to a diminutive dwarf. Tradition-ally, they have four digits on each hand and foot, as well as a tail. Sometimes it's said they turn to stone in sunlight or that they eat human flesh. The creatures originate from Scandina-via but have been rolled into the myths and stories of cultures with similar creatures throughout the Western world, just like fairies and elves. These days, you're more likely to see the term online, as a name for anonymous internet commenters who sow trouble for their own perverse pleasure—the scariest mon-sters of all.

The trolls in Mount Horeb, Wisconsin, aren't giants or human-eaters or internet jerks. They range in size from two feet tall to the size of an adult human, with cartoony features, old-fashioned clothes, and a general folksiness about them. They're not native to the town, though. Mount Horeb was orig-inally settled by the English in the mid-nineteenth century, but within a few decades, the town, like much of Wisconsin, expe-rienced a large influx of Norwegian immigrants. How trolls themselves got to Mount Horeb, though, involves a gift shop, some truckers, and the golden era of mother-in-law jokes.

In 1966, a store called Open House Imports opened in a quaint Victorian on Main Street. Its specialty was Scandinavian merchandise. A few years later, it imported some troll statues and placed them on its front lawn like so many garden gnomes. You'd think the rest of the story would be that those trolls just caught on until Mount Horeb was a troll fest, but the transformation was more calculated than that. It was a reaction to a looming economic disaster. In the 1980s, the main highway, which originally went directly through Mount Horeb, was diverted around the town. The local businesses were worried that the bypass meant being bypassed, so they put their heads together to figure out a way to lure drivers back into town. That's when they remembered the truckers.

Back when the main road shot through Main Street, passing truckers would use the trolls in front of Open House Imports as a waymark and a joke, coughing into their CB radios to each other, "I just passed your mother-in-law on Highway 18/151." The people of Mount Horeb thought that if trolls could grab the attention of road-hypnotized long-haulers, maybe they could draw others to town, too. Plus, it was a way to honor the Norwegian part of the town's heritage: two birds with one troll.

The leaders of Mount Horeb started commissioning wooden troll sculptures from a local artist named Michael Feeney. These troll statues varied in size and were depicted in a range of occupations such as gardening or feeding chickens or playing instruments. A mayor troll presents a key to the city. A peddler troll bears a pack of wares on its back as tall as the troll itself. Another holds an ice cream cone in its hand, ready for a brain freeze. An accordion-playing troll statue was once serenaded by a bus full of Norwegian accordion players passing through town in an impromptu twenty-minute concert. These trolls were placed outside and inside businesses along Main Street like so many live trolls turned to stone in the sunlight. The town rebranded the street the Trollway, and a phenomenon was born.

Today some three dozen trolls populate the Trollway. The town proudly proclaims on its website (where you can partake in a virtual troll hunt): "Come for the trolls. Stay for the community." Mount Horeb hosts multiple troll-themed events every year, and even when a downtown event isn't troll-themed, it still is, because you can't throw a rock without hitting a troll. A costumed character named Jorgen the Troll often shows up, too. They've even trademarked the phrase "Troll Capital of the World." And they're not done. More wooden statues are regularly added to the Trollway, as Mount Horeb continues to troll for tourists.

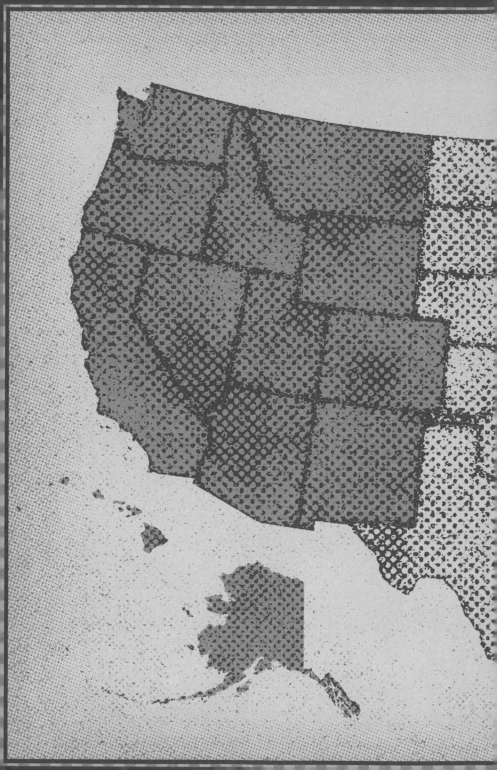

PART IV:
THE WEST

Bigfoot has been kind of a pain in my ass throughout this book. It's been seen everywhere, in every state, and celebrated in places that have much more interesting and unique creatures within their borders. I mean, there's no reason for states like Georgia, Massachusetts, and West Virginia to have bigfoot museums, but they do. But now, finally, we're in the region of the country where bigfoot obsession is the most legitimate: the West. It named the beast, made it famous, and it almost has more bigfoot sites than bigfoot sightings. They need a museum dedicated to all of their bigfoot museums. But the West has plenty of other fascinating cryptids scampering through that forest of tall furry legs—aliens and miniature beings and living pants. Rabbit-deer hybrids. Man-bats. Even dinosaurs. They all deserve their day in the western sun. But, yeah, bigfoot.

—California Bigfoot —

THE FIRST STEPS OF A MONSTER

TYPE: Humanoid	**YEAR NAMED:** 1958
DESCRIPTION: 6–8 feet tall, 300–400 pounds, bipedal, dark fur	**BIGFOOT FACT:** Bigfoot prints were first reported in California

California, and more specifically northern California, has three claims to being allowed to paint The Bigfoot State on its welcome signs. It found the brute. It named the brute. It filmed the brute. That's...a pretty strong case.

Bigfoot in its current form, that of a giant furry primate, is a relatively new phenomenon. Stories of wild men and giants permeate the histories and legends of most cultures, but none of them quite correspond to the bigfoot that we all know and love and adorn our beef jerky packaging with. Nor was bigfoot always the unofficial mascot of cryptozoology that it is today. In the early to mid-twentieth century, the yeti/abominable snowman of the Himalayas was all the rage in cryptid circles. But that was a faraway monster. A monster for intrepid survivalists and explorers. On this side of the world, the North American sasquatch got some press here and there, but it was highly localized to western Canada and was described more as a giant human than a giant ape, one that spoke and wore clothes and lived in villages.

A man named William Roe almost singlehandedly turned the sasquatch into a giant hairy primate with one encounter. While hiking in the woods of Alberta in the fall of 1955, he came across a large creature, six feet tall, 300 pounds, with short, dark, silver-tipped hair all over its body, including its face, which made it look, according to the affidavit that he signed two year later, like "an animal as much as a human." And it had breasts. The creature squatted in a clearing eating leaves. But that creature still wasn't called Bigfoot.

Bigfoot wasn't christened until 1958. Andrew Genzoli, a journalist for the *Humboldt Times* of Eureka, California, received a report that loggers on a road project in Bluff Creek, California, had been finding oversized humanlike footprints in the loose soil around their worksites. Genzoli wrote about them, including the fact that the workers called the creature who made them Bigfoot. And a star was born. The new name for the potentially older creature worked like a rebrand, not just for Bigfoot but for cryptozoology as a whole. Cryptids went from exotic creatures on snowy Himalayan mountains and faraway Scottish lochs to something that you could possibly find in the woods behind your house. And its name, Bigfoot, was chummy enough that it wasn't too scary.

And then it was caught on video. Maybe. In October 1967, cowboys Roger Patterson and Bob Gimlin jumped on their horses and headed to the forests around Bluff Creek, the location of the footprints that were found a decade earlier, with the specific purpose of finding and filming Bigfoot. And they did, depending on who you believe. The one-minute, shaky 16mm footage shows a large, hairy bigfoot with breasts striding heavily alongside Bluff Creek, only acknowledging its paparazzi with a single glance over its shoulder.

The video captured in Bluff Creek went on to define Bigfoot in American culture (although we turned it male because, I don't know, of course we did). In turn, Bigfoot has come to define Willow Creek, a town about twenty-five miles from the sighting, and the place where Patterson and Gimlin mailed off the film of the encounter to be developed. Today, fifty-five years after the Patterson-Gimlin footage and sixty-five years after the coinage of the word *bigfoot*, Willow Creek has become Bigfoot Central.

The Willow Creek-China Flat Museum is technically a local history museum, but its local history includes Bigfoot, and it knows who its star is. A twenty-five-foot-tall wooden Bigfoot statue stands out front, and a Bigfoot exhibit inside is full of footprint casts, pictures, and everything else Bigfoot-related. But really, the whole town is a bigfoot museum. Especially during Bigfoot Daze, a festival it hosts every year.

Oh, and every business in Willow Creek honors Bigfoot as if by law. There's a Bigfoot Steakhouse. A Bigfoot Motel. A Bigfoot Burgers. A Bigfoot lawnmower store. Even franchises that can't name themselves after the cryptid still tout him: the Ace Hardware has a wraparound mural on its exterior showing Bigfoot helping humans farm and build houses. The Patriot gas station has a statue and a mural of Bigfoot. You could spend a week in Willow Creek and only do bigfoot stuff, without ever setting foot in a forest.

And that's just in Willow Creek. I would need a whole book to catalog bigfoot in California alone, and I'm not letting the beast take over this one, although we'll see it a couple more times before the end.

-Fresno Nightcrawler-

THESE PANTS WERE MADE
FOR WALKING

TYPE:	EARLIEST SIGHTING:
Alien	2007
LOCATION:	**SIZE:**
Fresno, California	3 feet tall

This is the entry you've been waiting for: the weirdest one in the entire book. Weirder than New Hampshire's Derry Fairy and Iowa's Van Meter Visitor combined. Weird enough that it deserves commemoration of some sort. I'm talking about the Fresno nightcrawler: a mysterious twenty-first-century cryptid the sole evidence of which is video footage that rivals the famous Patterson-Gimlin bigfoot footage—in creepiness at least, if not in renown.

The security cam footage is low-res, grainy, blurry, obviously VHS, obviously night vision. A digital counter starting at 12:41:33 counts up at the bottom of the screen. The video reveals a small stretch of fenced-in front lawn with a single tree at the left side of the frame. Beyond the tree, movement; difficult to make out at first, as defects in the video distort and obfuscate the source of that movement like the thing is warping reality around itself. Quickly, the movement resolves into a figure. It's a thin, white column maybe three feet tall casting a thin column of dark shadow. It moves diagonally across the lawn, but it's difficult to see how it's moving at that resolution. It pauses for a moment at the bottom of the frame, and then disappears beyond. Five seconds later, at 12:46:47, a second, similar form follows the same pattern, although faster, with this column separating itself into a pair of thin, white legs—and that's it. No torso, no visible head, no arms: just a pair of legs strutting awkwardly across the frame and the lawn. The sentient legs are covered in what appears to be loose white cloth or skin. Overall, it's reminiscent of the haunted pants in Dr. Seuss's *What Was I Scared Of?*

The video dates to 2007 and was taken by a man known only as Jose. He had set up a closed-circuit video system on the front lawn of his home in Fresno, California, because his house had been burgled before. That night he heard the neighborhood dogs barking madly and wanted to see if his camera had picked up the source of their disturbance. It had. And now it was the source of *his* disturbance.

Jose called the television network Univision to tell them about the footage. They dispatched a crew who looked at the footage, but couldn't get the tape out of the VCR. They recorded the footage off Jose's monitor with a video camera, further lowering the quality of the video. Then they called in local paranormal expert Michael Banti in the hope he'd identify the strange pants as extraterrestrial. Banti stayed uncommitted, but also stayed on the case. He got a copy of the footage and presented it at a convention, projecting it onto a screen. That presentation was recorded and eventually uploaded to YouTube, all the replication stripping the video of any illuminating details.

The profile of the bipedal creatures was raised when a show called *Fact or Faked: Paranormal* aired an episode about them on the Syfy channel in 2010. This show gave the creatures the name Fresno nightcrawlers, despite neither one of them crawling in the clip. The show also tried to replicate the footage on Jose's property with a puppet and then a child in a sheet. They were unable to deem the footage either fact or faked.

After the episode aired, more videos of the nightcrawlers surfaced, most obvious pranks, although one purportedly taken in Yosemite National Park on another security cam seems to show clearer video of a pair of Fresno nightcrawlers striding past like half-complete humanoids. The clearer footage doesn't offer any better explanation of their identity.

The original footage is gone. Jose died a few years after it was taken. The Fresno nightcrawlers' entire story is contained in that single, blurry, overly replicated video. No legend accompanies it, either urban or ancient. There are no physical encounters to add to the case file. The only lesson to learn here is that Dr. Seuss was right: sentient pants are terrifying.

– Kodiak Dinosaur –

MY CRYPTID CAN EAT YOUR CRYPTID

TYPE:	EARLIEST SIGHTING:
Aquatic-saurian	1969
LOCATION:	SIZE:
Kodiak Archipelago, Alaska	200 feet long

Alaska is the biggest state, so I expect a big cryptid from it: bigger than a bigfoot, bigger than a thunderbird, bigger than a lake monster. And it's said to hide all those creatures and more somewhere within its vast wilderness. But when it comes to gargantuan, supersized, colossal, gigantic, massive cryptids, Alaska does not disappoint. In fact, it might have the largest cryptid on the entire cryptid map with the Kodiak Dinosaur.

On April 15, 1969, a sixty-five-foot-long shrimp boat called the *Mylark* was trawling for small crustaceans in the Raspberry Straits, which wend through the Kodiak Archipelago off the southern shore of the state. The boat was captained by Chet Peterson, and what he and his crew found was not a shrimp, in either sense of the word.

When the sonar alarm sounded, it detected something 55 fathoms (330 feet) below. Something big. Something approaching 200 feet long. The area's home to the largest creature that has ever called the planet home, the blue whale, but those cetaceans max out at about half that length, which meant whatever was down there just knocked the blue whale down to second place. Besides, the shape returned on the sonar was no whale, not with its leglike flippers, its long neck ending in a blunt head, and its long tapering tail. This seemed to be a massive aquatic reptile millions of years past its expiration date.

To put the size of the Kodiak Dinosaur in perspective, the Walgren Lake Monster of Nebraska is estimated at around 40 to 100 feet long. Champ, out in Lake Champlain in Vermont/New York, is 15 to 50 feet, and the Loch Ness Monster 10 to 45 feet. At two-thirds the length of a football field, the Kodiak Dinosaur would barely fit in some of the lakes that boast lake monsters.

When the *Mylark* returned to shore, the crew told their story and the local *Kodiak Mirror* put it in print, which is how Ivan T. Sanderson heard about it. Sanderson was a British biologist and paranormalist who would become one of the founding fathers of cryptozoology. He got his hands on the strip of graph paper that the sonar printed the image on and immediately became an evangelist for the sighting. He first took it to the Norwegian company that had made the sonar, a Simrad EH2A, a cutting-edge device imported to the US through a subsidiary named Supervisors, Incorporated. They claimed that the image had been tampered with.

Undeterred, Sanderson talked to more than a dozen other maritime technology experts, who validated the sonar image as unmanipulated. He concluded that the image showed a real monster, something prehistoric and now historic. His story, "Alaska's Sea Monster," made the cover of *Argosy* magazine in June 1970. In it, he concluded, "I for one am convinced that (1) Simrad is not faulty (2) the echogram is perfectly authentic and (3) somewhere in the icy waters of the southern coast of Alaska there's at least one monstrous marine long neck swimming around—and who knows how many more?"

Since then, although several smaller potential sea monsters have been sighted around Alaska, a monster large enough to be another Kodiak Dinosaur wasn't spotted for another half century. This time it was discovered not by sonar but by naked eyeballs (held wide open in terror). In 2002, three boatsmen, Dave Little, Tollef Monsen, and a third unnamed crewperson, set off in a 22-foot skiff to net salmon in the waters off Kodiak Island. It was daytime, which gave them a good view of the massive head that suddenly broke the water at the port bow. According to the Kodiak Maritime Museum, Monsen described it this way: "There's this neck and head, and it wasn't like your hands around the neck big, it was like your arms around the neck big." Little described it as dark and moving but was unable to give any more details because he had been driving. He didn't get a chance for a second look because as soon as the beast appeared, it dove back under.

As a coda, John Carlsen, a representative of the company that made the Simrad that first detected the beast, would later admit that after Sanderson's article came out, orders for the device rose exponentially. Everybody wanted a machine that could find a sea monster. Unfortunately for them, the company didn't launch a sea monster marketing campaign for the device, but they did stop actively discouraging (and possibly started encouraging) that interpretation of the *Mylark's* sonar readout.

And you know who else should launch a sea monster marketing campaign? Alaska itself. Why shouldn't Alaska tout its giant? They could sell bumper stickers that read MY CRYPTID CAN EAT YOUR CRYPTID. Put up welcome signs that say HOME OF THE WORLD'S BIGGEST BEAST. Print shirts with the Simrad image on them. They should really embrace this thing—even if they can't get their arms around its neck.

«———◆———»

– Skinwalker –

WEREWOLF WITCHES

TYPE:	EARLIEST SIGHTING:
Canine-humanoid	Prehistory
LOCATION:	**NOTABLE FEATURE:**
Southwest US, particularly Arizona	Shapeshifter

"That's a door between worlds. My people believe we entered our current world through something like this. It's also how the skinwalkers get around. Those are our boogeymen," the guide explained to me. His name was Ryan. He was a young, laid-back Navajo man earning cash as a tour guide while studying music theory at college. He was leading a group of us through Upper Antelope Canyon in Arizona. The size of my tip at the end of the tour was completely in proportion to the beauty of those four sentences.

Skinwalkers are humans that change into animals, often wolves. Because of that, they've been lumped into the werewolf category of horror stories and the dogman/wolfman category of cryptids by settlers. Whether a creature is identified as a skinwalker versus a dogman or wolfman often depends on the state where they're seen—skinwalkers are known throughout the Southwest—and the size of the local Navajo population. However, skinwalkers aren't tragic characters turned lupine against their will, as in horror stories, nor are they some species of evolutionarily confusing creature, as in cryptid legends. Skinwalkers want to be monsters.

In Navajo stories, skinwalkers are evil beings. Witches. Human sorcerers of dark magic who attain their status by committing specific atrocities such as murdering a family member. Their defining characteristic is that they can shapeshift into other creatures, like foxes and coyotes. But mostly they turn into wolves. And unlike other humanoid canines, they can travel via magical doors between worlds, one of which is in Upper Antelope Canyon.

Antelope Canyon is a 660-foot-long slot canyon, a thin passageway created by flowing water on Navajo land in Arizona. It can only be accessed when led by a Navajo guide. The entrance to the upper canyon is in an outcropping of sandstone about 120 feet high with an ominous vertical opening slitting its face. Inside that opening, a winding passage varies in width from several yards to a couple chest-widths wide. The floor is covered with a thin layer of fine sand. Above, the sliver of light that is the top of the crevice is often blocked by twists in the rock wall.

It was beautiful. Enough light filtered in to set a comfortable, ethereal mood, and the walls were gorgeous, almost glowing pink and orange and shaped like frozen waves, as if someone had sculpted the soft sandstone with a cake icing tool. In reality, it was water that had done all the sculpting. Even though the place was bone dry on our visit, it is extremely prone to flash floods. The idea was terrifying even without the werewolf witches: being trapped in that claustrophobic space, underwater, knocked against all the beautiful whorls and outcrops of rock. And that wasn't just paranoia—people have drowned in Antelope Canyon. In 1997, eleven succumbed to a flash flood there. In 2010, during another flash flood, a group was able to get to safety, but was stranded until the waters abated.

The skinwalker door that Ryan had drawn my attention to was a flat section of rock, about six feet tall, inset into the wall and rounded at the top. It's nothing I would have noticed on my own, but once pointed out, it did seem like all it needed was a knob. Modern stories of skinwalker encounters don't involve portals, and, of course, Ryan might have just been having a bit of fun with a wide-eyed tourist, as many Navajo find the subject to be taboo and don't like to discuss skinwalkers, especially with outsiders.

In 1987, skinwalkers burst into the wider public consciousness when they were used as a defense in a murder trial in Flagstaff, Arizona. The body of a forty-year-old Navajo woman named Sarah Saganitso was found behind the hospital where she worked. A former English professor at Northern Arizona University named George Abney was accused, arrested, and taken to trial. The defense argued that a skinwalker had killed Saganitso, based on the fact that she was Navajo and found with a broken stick across her throat and a clump of graveyard grass near her truck. The defense claimed the two objects were evidence of a skinwalker ritual. Abney was at first found guilty, but then acquitted a year later.

Skinwalkers have continued to capture people's imaginations ever since. In 2021, a clip was released on TikTok that purported to show a strange, skeletal creature jumping from a grassy patch of wilderness. It gathered six million views and tons of comments hypothesizing that the creature was a skinwalker. In fact, clips with the hashtag #skinwalker have a total of more than a billion views on that social media platform, mostly thanks to one Navajo creator named John Soto, who raised the profile of the creature when in fall 2020 he posted a series of videos of himself looking for skinwalkers on his Arizona property that went viral and garnered millions of views.

It's an ancient evil, a horror story, a cryptid, a meme. The skinwalker is a surprisingly versatile monster. And if you want to up your chances of finding one, I can take you to its front door.

– Slide-Rock Bolter –

LANDSLIDE TRANSMOGRIFIED

TYPE:	EARLIEST SIGHTING:
Cetacean	19th century
LOCATION:	NOTABLE FEATURE:
Rocky Mountains, Colorado	Hooked tail

You hear a rumble on the mountain above you; feel a vibration that shakes the ground. You quickly make peace with your fate as you turn, expecting your final earthly sight to be an ominous cloud of crushing rock and choking soil racing down the mountain, both your killer and your gravedigger. Instead you see something else sliding down the mountain. It looks like a...whale? You still die, though. Just confused. And you're eaten instead of crushed: by a slide-rock bolter.

The original source of this Colorado creature is William T. Cox's *Fearsome Creatures of the Lumberwoods*, published in 1910. In that work, which I've referenced a couple times in this book, Cox wanted to preserve the lore of what he feared was a vanishing species—the lumberjack, and especially the strange creatures and monsters they saw in the dark, isolated woods while logging. It's unknown how many of the twenty creatures in his book are actual tales he heard from burly men with axes or creatures he just made up, but most of the animals within appear for the first time in the written record there, including

the magnificent slide-rock bolter.

The slide-rock bolter is a large, carnivorous land whale with small eyes, a wide mouth, and a hooked tail that it uses to anchor itself to the sides of mountains. The creature's coloration and skin texture are perfect camouflage for the environment, making it look to all the world like a flank of mountain. When it spots prey (which Cox writes are often tourists), it lets go of the mountain. Its weight, the steep incline, and lubricating saliva streaming from its mouth combine to give it the speed of a landslide as it shoots downhill, flattening trees, pulverizing boulders, and scooping up edible animals with the effortlessness of one of its ocean cousins sifting krill. It then uses inertia to ascend the next incline like a skateboarder in a half-pipe, where it flips around and anchors its tail to wait for its next victims.

The only specific story Cox tells of a slide-rock bolter is one in which a forest ranger kills one of the massive beasts on the slopes of Lizard Head, a mountain in the southwest corner of the state. The ranger dresses a dummy like a tourist (complete with expensive coat and field guide) and stuffs it full of explosives. The slide-rock bolter takes the bait and slide-bolts down Lizard Head to swallow the dummy. The fake tourist explodes in the creature's mouth, scattering blubber across the landscape and flattening half of the nearby town of Rico.

Rico was a nineteenth-century mining town focused on extracting gold and silver from them thar hills. History doesn't say it was flattened by falling cryptid pieces (it also doesn't *not* say that), but after the mines dried up and the industry was abandoned, many of the buildings decayed into debris. Some have hypothesized that the real connection between the slide-rock bolter and Rico was that the lumberjacks, who moved in when logging replaced mining, saw wide trails of rubble in the mountains, as well as other environmental damage from mining, which looked a lot like the trails of a slide-rock bolter.

Now that you've heard this tale, and before we write off William T. Cox as a fantasist, it should be stated that the man knew his wilderness. He was the State Forester of Minnesota and Commissioner of Conservation and spent his life working with governments to manage forests throughout the US, Canada, and Brazil.

No other state has anything close to this creature. A cryptid avalanche like this one could only live in a place like Colorado, with its towering, steep mountains. Of course, instead of celebrating this unique beast, Colorado has a Sasquatch Outpost Museum in Bailey. But if you ever find yourself among the peaks of Colorado's Rocky Mountains, and you see a cleared path shaved down a mountainside, sure, maybe it was for telephone wires or a ski slope. Maybe a landslide scoured it clean. Or maybe it's evidence of a slide-rock bolter in action, in which case, maybe look out behind you.

— Menehune —

ELFIN ENGINEERS

TYPE:	EARLIEST SIGHTING:
Humanoid	Prehistory
LOCATION:	**SIZE:**
Kauai, Hawaii	2–3 feet tall, possibly as small as 6 inches

In European folklore, elves and brownies and other diminutive fay folk make toys and shoes and do chores around human houses. They're nice little beings: quaint, perfect fodder for pleasant children's stories. But in Hawaii, the island imps are no mere cobblers and maids. They're sophisticated architects and engineers—with a vengeful streak.

In native Hawaiian lore, Menehune are miniature humans, about two or three feet tall, although some say they are as small as six inches. The inconsistency might be because the cryptid-beings can only be seen by their descendants, although anyone can hear them hum as they work. The story of their origins is equally inconsistent. Some believe they are the original inhabitants of the Hawaiian Islands but were chased into hiding by the much larger Tahitian settlers around 1100 (*Menehune* means something like "commoner" in Tahitian). Some say they are supernatural entities that have always lived in the forests and caves and hills of the archipelago. Some even say they are a tribe of Judah (Hawaiian and Biblical lore contain interesting parallels). But if you make a formal request to the Menehune, and you treat them right, they will build you bridges and temples, and they will do it in a single night. In fact, they only work at night, and they won't start a project they can't finish in a single night (which is a technicality because they can finish any project in a night, as long as they aren't interrupted).

The evidence of their skills can be found mostly on Kauai, the middle-sized island of the main eight. There they built the Alekoko Fishpond (also known as the Menehune Fishpond), a 1,000-year-old dam made of lava rock. The dam is 900 feet long and five feet high and segments a portion of the Huleia River. It was purportedly built to provide fish for Hawaiian royalty. It has gaps in its construction and, according to the story, that's because the Menehune were interrupted by two siblings of the royal family who spied on their work. The Menehune turned them both into stone pillars and left the site unfinished.

Presumably no one interrupted their work on the Kikiaola Ditch, which they did finish, and without any casualties. Kikiaola Ditch is an extremely rare example of a stone-lined irrigation ditch connected to the Waimea River. It dates back to at least the thirteenth century, although only a fraction of it survives. The Menehune are also credited for the Poliahu Heiau, a temple that is now a ruin. Although most of their work is found on Kauai, you can also find remnants of their work on other islands—for instance, the Ulupō Heiau, an ancient temple on Oahu, and stone structures and figures on Necker Island, which was said to be the last refuge of the Menehune after the Tahitian settlers drove them out.

But the connecting of these historic sites with the Menehune aren't just oral traditions weaponized by tour guides to bulk out their spiel for lei-strangled tourists. Hawaii gives the small builders appropriate credit for their work. Most Menehune building sites have historic plaques built into them labeling them as the work of the little people.

The Menehune, along with many other legends of diminutive cryptid-beings around the world, got a boost in 2003 when the skeleton of a three-foot-tall human ancestor species was found in a cave on the island of Flores in Indonesia. Its scientific name was *Homo floresiensis*, but it got a nickname, too. Unfortunately, it wasn't Menehune, but Hobbit, as the world was in thrall of the final installment of Peter Jackson's *Lord of the Rings* movie trilogy at the time.

But that's fine. Honestly, they don't even need the plaques on their feats of engineering. It's all about the work for the Menehune. As long as you don't interrupt them.

– Washington Bigfoot –

MOST BIGFOOT PER SQUARE FOOT

TYPE:
Humanoid

BIGFOOT FACT 1:
Washington has more
bigfoot sightings than
any other state

BIGFOOT FACT 2:
Washington has the
biggest bigfoot statue in
the country

If California can claim both naming and filming Bigfoot, what's left for the other states of the Pacific Northwest to claim? When it comes to Washington, a lot. For instance, according to the Bigfoot Field Researchers Organization, Washington has the most bigfoot sightings of any state, at 2,032. That's about 400 more sightings than California, despite the latter being more than two times the size of America's corner pocket. Washington also claims the world's tallest bigfoot statue, the most terrifying bigfoot story, and, maybe most important, *Harry and the Hendersons*.

Let's start with that statue. It stands outside the North Fork Survivors Gift Shop in the town of Toutle. It's twenty-eight feet tall, which is the tallest statue of a bigfoot in any medium in the entire country. And it's made out of cement mixed with ashes from the 1980 eruption of nearby Mount St. Helens. The bigfoot is smiling and holding onto a tree. Some call it the Bigfoot Memorial, due to the legend that the eruption of Mount St. Helens (the same eruption that unleashed batsquatch, see page

248) killed the bigfoot. The statue was built in the early 1990s by an artist named Beverly Roberts. A few big footsteps away from the statue is an A-frame house half buried in the ground from the river of mud and ash that flooded the area during the eruption. A bigfoot and a buried house: You can't ask for much more from an attraction.

No statue marks the site of one of the scariest bigfoot stories in the lore, regardless of state. On the eastern side of Mount St. Helens is Ape Canyon, which is named for a horrifying battle that happened there in 1924. A group of gold prospectors that included Fred Beck, Gabe Lefever, John Peterson, Marion Smith, and Smith's son Roy erected a cabin in the canyon while they searched for gold. At one point, while walking through the woods, they encountered a trio of dark-haired, 7-foot-tall, 400-pound bigfoot. Beck fired his rifle, hitting one and knocking it off a cliff. Then they got out of there. That night, while sleeping in the cabin, the group felt the structure shake as boulders pummeled it and large bodies threw themselves against it. The avenging bigfoot even ripped open the roof and threw stones inside, beaning Beck into unconsciousness. Thanks to their firearms, the group was able to survive until morning, when the bigfoot all gave up and returned to the forest. The miners left fast. Another version of the story is that the apes attacked the cabin unprovoked, and Beck didn't shoot one off a cliff until the end of the siege.

Either way, the prospectors told their story to the authorities, and two rangers with the US Forest Service, J. H. Huffman and William Welch, hiked out to the cabin to investigate. Apparently, they weren't too impressed with what they found. They believed the attack had been staged, with the rocks deliberately placed around the cabin and the footprints faked. Still, the story stuck around to such a degree that the place became known as Ape Canyon.

A much less terrifying (and even more famous) bigfoot story is *Harry and the Hendersons*. The 1987 comedy film starring John Lithgow and Melinda Dillon as the Hendersons and Kevin Peter Hall as Harry is about a family that adopts a bigfoot after hitting it with their car. The movie was both set and shot in Washington. Viewers fell in love with this goofy, gentle bigfoot, and the movie won an Oscar and spun off into a television series. Harry's high forehead, large teeth, and beard inspired countless statues, including the Dahl Bigfoot of South Dakota (see page 185). One of the filming locations, a small shack in the town of Gold Bar where Lithgow talked to a bigfoot hunter played by Don Ameche, has been commemorated with a fourteen-foot-tall wooden statue of a bigfoot out front.

I guess when you're the state with the most bigfoot encounters, you can have a range that goes from Ape Canyon home invaders to a furry, friendly movie star.

The Billion Names of Bigfoot

Every state in the country has had a bigfoot sighting, but its name is rarely bigfoot. In New Hampshire, big hairy hominids are called wood devils. In Missouri, it's Momo (short for Missouri Monster). Ohio has grassmen. Alabama has White Thang. In Louisiana, it's the Honey Island Swamp Monster. In North Carolina, they've got Knobby. New Jersey has Big Red Eye. Why so many different names?

The reason goes back to how bigfoot were originally named. The term *bigfoot* didn't step onto the scene until 1958. Before that, giant hairy hominids weren't really a North American thing. The yeti lived in the Himalayas, and the term *sasquatch* had been around in the Pacific Northwest and Western Canada since the 1920s, but it was an anglicized term from a Halkomelem word that referred to giant humans who could talk and wore clothes and lived in villages.

In 1958, a journalist named Andrew Genzolia reported that loggers in Bluff Creek, California, had found giant human footprints at their worksite. Genzolia naturally named the unseen creature that had made them bigfoot, since that's all anyone knew about the creature.

The rest of the country wouldn't wake up to hairy giants in their forests until the 1970s, but each of those later-century encounters invariably started with a sighting of the beast itself. And when a person witnesses a massive, muscular creature covered in dark hair with glowing eyes, they don't think about the size of its feet. They just think about the monster.

Had those loggers in California actually seen a monster in 1958 instead of just footprints, it may have been reported as the Bluff Creek Monster, and we would never have had the term bigfoot. And how sad would that be?

– Batsquatch –

BIGFOOT WITH WINGS

TYPE: Aerial-humanoid	**EARLIEST SIGHTING:** 1994
LOCATION: Mount St. Helens and Mount Rainier, Washington	**SIZE:** 9 feet tall

The people of the state of Washington, while still big into bigfoot, have improved and one-upped that mascot of the Pacific Northwest with a single amazing tweak. Taking a cue from Red Bull, from Christmas bells, from Daedalus, and from the Wright Brothers, Washington gave the bigfoot wings—and then gave it the absurdly awesome name of batsquatch. The flying hairy humanoid is the West Coast version of Mothman, but jacked. And I keep giving credit to the people of Washington for the beast and its name, but really it was mostly the fine work of one teenager.

That's right—this cryptid story starts yet again with a teenager in a car at night. This time, it's eighteen-year-old Brian Canfield in his pickup truck, and it's April 1994, about 9:30 p.m., in an isolated part of the state outside of Tacoma. He was heading home to a place called Camp One, in the foothills of Mount Rainier. The mountain loomed nearby, covering the darkness of the night sky with its own darkness. It wasn't a great place for one's truck to break down under normal circumstances, but Canfield quickly discovered an abnormal circumstance to boot. Before he could even curse and hit the steering wheel of his dead truck, something large dropped heavily in front of the truck, pinned by its still working headlamps. The thing was a broad-shouldered, nine-foot-tall humanoid with big yellow eyes, a mouth full of sharp teeth, and tufted ears. It had clawed feet and a wolf-like face and was covered with fur a shade of blue that Canfield compared to the NBC Peacock.

"It was standing there staring at me, like it was resting, like it didn't know what to think," Canfield told a reporter from the *News Tribune* out of Tacoma a few days later. "I was scared. It raised the hair on me. I didn't feel threatened. I just felt out of place." After a few minutes of that strange standoff, the creature spread wings as wide as the two-lane road and took off into the night sky toward Mount Rainier, its wings beating the air so hard that it rocked the truck, which started again as soon as the beast was swallowed by the night.

Canfield raced home and told his parents, who were worried enough by their son's flustered state that his father grabbed a gun, a camera, and a neighbor and returned to the spot. They found nothing but a lonely stretch of dark road. But that moment was all the creature needed to secure its legacy. Canfield sketched an image of what he had seen, assisted by some of his high school friends, who also helped name it batsquatch.

And that's really the only clear sighting of batsquatch in Washington. In Linda S. Godfrey's book *American Monsters*, she does tell the story of a Tacoma family who reported multiple encounters on their property in July 2011 with a strange, gray, smooth-skinned bat that had a wingspan of four feet. It made monkey-like noises and would glide toward them in the night. This was notable since it was in Tacoma (there are bats with wingspans of up to five feet, but only in the Philippines), but the description hardly sounds like Canfield's batsquatch, unless it was a deformed juvenile.

Still, an entire mythology has evolved out of that single sighting. It's said that the creature (or creatures) once lived at Mount St. Helens, maybe in hibernation, maybe in isolation, but only until the volcano's eruption in 1980 drove them from their hiding place until they found a new home at Mount Rainier. It's not the first time Washington has roped Mount St. Helens into its cryptid lore—another story goes that the blast actually killed off all the bigfoot.

Batsquatch hasn't yet been commemorated by the state like its wingless cousin has, but Washington better consider it quickly. Since Canfield's encounter popularized batsquatch, there have been sightings of batsquatch-like creatures in California, Texas, Missouri, Pennsylvania, Illinois, and Wisconsin. And the number one search result for it on Google is the Batsquatch IPA from Rogue Brewing—headquartered next door in Oregon.

Sharlie

REBRANDING A BEAST

TYPE:	EARLIEST SIGHTING:
Aquatic	1920
LOCATION:	SIZE:
McCall, Idaho	35 feet long

Most water monsters get their names from the body of
water they inhabit—Champ in Vermont's Lake Champlain,
Altamaha-ha in Georgia's Altamaha River, Chessie in Maryland's Chesapeake Bay. Not the monster of Payette Lake in
McCall, Idaho, though, which you'd think would be christened
Patty. Nope. It's Sharlie—Sharlie the Lake Monster. And it got
that name from a newspaper contest, revealing that maybe the
people of McCall are a little more cynical about their lake monster than other lake monster communities.

McCall was established as a logger settlement back in the
late nineteenth century, nestled among the mountains and
forests of what would eventually become Payette National
Forest. In 1920, a logger crew saw a log floating in the clear
water of Payette Lake—or what they thought was a log, until
it started moving and swimming in a way that logs don't. Tales
of the large, serpentine creature in the lake were passed around
the camps on the dark, timber-shadowed shores of those 5,330
acres of pristine glacial water. Over the decades, the area's economy shifted from felling trees to drawing tourists. And nothing

draws the tourists like a lake monster.

The beast received its first name in 1944, when it was seen by a group of people near a section of the lake called the Narrows. The consensus was that it had the head of a dinosaur with a big jaw, the humps of a camel, and was more than thirty-five feet long. It was also described as having "shell-like skin," which is unclear but probably referred to its scaly texture. The story went national, and the monster was dubbed Slimy Slim by *Time* magazine.

People flocked to McCall from all around, from ardent monster hunters to casual tourists who were drawn to the town's natural beauty and outdoor recreation. From that point on, just about every summer, somebody saw the reptilian humps or head of Slimy Slim in the water. Many locals pretended it was only silly tourists who saw the creature, that it was less a byproduct of nature and more, as the *Idaho Statesman* put it, a "byproduct of the cocktail hour." But the truth was that locals saw the beast, too.

But now that Slimy Slim was part of the lake's marketing campaign, did the people of McCall want it to be so . . . slimy? After all, Payette Lake is known for its crystal clear, refreshing glacier water, shaded by sweet-smelling pines. Locals didn't want their brand to be icky at all. In 1954, the *Payette Lakes Star* decided to rebrand the monster. It held a naming contest. Whoever came up with the best name, as decided by a panel of judges that included local politicians and entrepreneurs, would get $40 and be one of the few people in the world to have "named a monster" on their resume. The newspaper received some two hundred entries, not just from Idaho but from all over the country. Some of the name ideas were barely better than Slimy Slim, including Nobby Dick, Humpy, and Snorky.

The prize went to Leisle Hennefer Tury of Virginia, who was originally from Idaho. She suggested Sharlie, which was based on a popular catchphrase voiced by radio performer Jack Pearl beginning in the 1930s. He had a bit where he voiced a character named Baron Munchausen. The Baron would tell an unbelievable story, get called out on it, and respond in an exaggerated German accent, "Vas you dere, Sharlie?" ("Were you there, Charlie?"). Like I said, the people of McCall really got it. And if there's further proof of that needed, second place in the naming contest went to the suggestion Boon, as in "boon for the economy" (and also the name of the editor and publisher of the *Payette Lakes Star*).

These days, Sharlie sightings in the lake seem to be rarer but not completely extinct. And if you count Sharlie sightings outside the lake, there's still a couple every year. For instance, there's a Sharlie snow sculpture and parade float at the annual McCall Winter Carnival. There's also a year-round plastic statue at the local playground. Just don't call it Slimy Slim.

– Shunka Warak'in –

NOT YOUR AVERAGE WOLF

TYPE:	EARLIEST SIGHTING:
Canine	1886
LOCATION:	**SIZE:**
Ennis, Montana	4 feet long, 28 inches tall

Something has been preying on domesticated animals across the plains of Montana for centuries. It has been given many names over the years, below most of which burn angry red squiggly lines when typed into Microsoft Word: Shunka warak'in. Ringdocus. Guyasticutus. But it's also been called the Beast and the Rocky Mountain hyena—in fact, any name but wolf, although the creature could easily be called a wolf. Perhaps that's because wolves were extinct in the state for about half of the twentieth century, but that's a blip in the shunka warak'in's reign of terror. Whatever they are, they are known to attack dogs and cows and sheep and anything else served up on a fenced-in platter. If only we had a carcass, we could figure out what this creature is once and for all.

Oh, wait. Turns out, we do. It's on display in a museum in Montana. In 1886, in the Madison Valley of Montana, a settler named Israel Ammon Hutchins had a problem. Something was attacking his animals, and the animals of other farmers and ranchers in the area. Something dark and canine-like that screamed in the night like nothing he had ever heard. One morning he awoke to his dogs barking and jumped out of bed to find the canid chasing his geese. The beast had a dark coat, high shoulders, and a slanted back. Hutchins finally got a shot at it, but missed, killing one of his cows instead. The next time he got it in its sights, though, he missed the cow and killed the cryptid.

Hutchins traded the carcass to a businessman named Joseph Sherwood in exchange for a new cow. Sherwood was also a taxidermist, so he mounted the creature and showcased it in his combo grocery store/museum in Henry Lake, Idaho. He dubbed it a ringdocus, for reasons unknown. The ringdocus outlasted Sherwood and was on display at least into the 1980s. And then it disappeared. Dead cryptids can be as hard to find as live ones.

The only physical evidence of the existence of the stuffed ringdocus was a black and white photo of the beast published in 1977 in the autobiography of naturalist Ross Hutchins, the grandson of the original monster (and cow) slayer. In the photo, the creature looks wolf-like, but not quite like a wolf. Something about the shape of its face and arch of its back is different. The photo was captioned Guyasticutus, which some have offered is a cheeky name for something fake made to sell tickets.

The story of the creature and the frustrating disappearance of its corpse continued to circulate. Meanwhile, Lance Foster, a historic site preservationist, paranormal enthusiast, and member of the Ioway tribe, speculated that the beast could be a shunka warak'in, a canid non-wolf beast from Native American lore that would sneak into camps at night and make off with dogs (the name translates to "carries off dogs"). After one particularly fierce battle with a shunka warak'in, in which the tribe was victorious, they took pieces of its hide to place into sacred bundles that they wore during battle to make them as hard to kill as the shunka warak'in had been. The name took off after it was used by Loren Coleman in his book *Cryptozoology A to Z*.

Eventually, another of Israel Hutchins's grandsons, Jack Kirby, got on the case. He learned that after Sherwood's museum shut down, the entire taxidermy collection was donated to the Idaho Museum of Natural History in Pocatello, where it was all put in storage. Soon after that he learned that one of those taxidermied beasts under the dusty sheets was the shunka warak'in itself. It was four feet long and twenty-eight inches at the shoulder, dark gray in color, with a low head and sloping back. Vague stripes could be seen on its flanks.

Kirby was able to convince the museum to loan it to the Madison Valley History Museum in Ennis, Montana, where it's been on display for more than a decade. Kirby took it there himself, although he first stopped at his grandfather's grave to reunite the mortal enemies turned cryptozoology legends. Today, the creature is the museum's most popular exhibit. They just call it the Beast.

But what is it? The shunka warak'in of legend? A canine mutant? A wolf-dog hybrid, a dog-coyote hybrid, hyena, or hyena-hybrid? Canids are extremely malleable cross-breeders, as anyone who has seen a French pug knows. Or is it just a bad taxidermy mount? Only a DNA test could tell, and all interested parties have decided not to do that. The mystery of the shunka warak'in has gone on so long that nobody wants to risk solving it.

–Giant Sky Clam–

FLYING SAUCER CRYPTIDS

TYPE:	EARLIEST SIGHTING:
Aerial-alien	1925
LOCATION:	**SIZE:**
Battle Mountain, Nevada	8–30 feet in diameter

Put aside cryptozoology for a moment, and let's talk UFOs. Let's say you want to believe. You've decided that those strange lights in the night sky are not secret military aircraft, swamp gas, or misinterpretations of natural astral phenomena. You're firmly in camp "advanced extraterrestrial craft." I'm going to ask you to rethink that position once again: what if those saucer-shaped lights in the night sky are actually giant flying clams?

Flying Saucers magazine published a doozy of a letter in the reader reports section of its October 1959 issue. The author must have thought it to be a doozy, too, because he asked the magazine not to print his name, making it the only anonymous report in the entire section. Later, the account would be credited to a man named Don Wood Jr. Wood claimed a personal sighting in 1925 that he believed "solved most of these U.F.O. reports." He and three friends were flying what he called "Jennies" out in the Nevada desert. "Jenny" was the nickname of a boxy Curtis JN biplane originally used as a training plane in World War I. After the war, they were sold at extremely cheap prices on the private market, allowing pilots in these early days of aviation to own their own aircraft (the Wrights had only left Kitty Hawk soil two decades before).

These early-adopters were buzzing the buttes of Nevada when they landed atop what Wood called Flat Mesa, near the town of Battle Mountain. Flat Mesa is about 5,000 square feet with sheer cliff walls on all sides, and difficult to access by any other means than landing atop it, which means few, if any, humans had ever been up there before that point. There, Wood and company witnessed a drama that haunted him for decades, until he finally tried to exorcise the experience by writing to a small UFO magazine.

The pilots landed at one p.m. and got out to walk around. Not long after, something else landed. It skidded to a stop about thirty feet from the pilots. It was round and flat "like a saucer," about eight feet across. It had a shell-like carapace that Wood compared to mica. The top was wet-looking, the bottom reddish. They approached it, immediately recognizing the strange object as a living, organic thing ("So help me, this was an animal," wrote Wood). The top half of the shell rose and fell like it was breathing, revealing a six-inch gap all the way around. It seemed to be a giant mollusk—that had flown down from the sky.

Another unusual feature of the creature seemed to be an injury. A large chunk of the edge of the disc was missing, and the hole oozed a "metal looking froth." As they approached, the rising and falling of the top shell accelerated and the glider tried to take off, only making it a few inches into the air before dropping back to the ground. The men, thinking that they were agitating the creature, backed off. The glider stopped moving for about twenty minutes, at which point it continued its strange respiration-like movement. Then the thing started to glow everywhere except for the spot of the injury. Wood described the effect as "bright as all get out."

Then, the only thing that could have pulled the men's eyes away from a giant pulsating sky clam pulled their eyes away: a bigger pulsating sky clam. The shadow that suddenly blocked the desert sun was another living disc, this one about thirty feet in diameter, more than three times the size of the creature on the ground. The larger glider hovered over the smaller one and extended four "sucker-like tongues" which attached to the injured creature, like either a parent consoling a child or a predator finishing off its prey. They both glowed like mini-suns until they were hard to look at, before rising together and speeding away at what Wood estimated must have been about 1,000 miles per hour.

The men approached the spot where the original creature had lain and caught a whiff of a strong, foul odor. Up close, the metal froth it had left behind looked like thin metal wire. More had been exuded in a thirty-foot circle around it, matching up to the dimensions of the bigger glider, like it had exhaled the wire. The froth melted quickly in the sun, and the men jumped back in their Jennies and flew off.

Stories of undiscovered sky creatures appear here and there in cryptid lore, especially in the early days of flight when this new environment was still a mystery to Earth-bound humans. Ideas have been offered about giant invisible amoebas and transparent flying manta rays populating the skies, but nothing as detailed as Wood's account, most of which is still a mystery. What were those things? Were they native to Nevada or extra-terrestrial visitors themselves? Are they really the answer to mysterious lights in the sky? Although the bigger mystery of the entire story might be that chunk missing from the first creature: What up there is feeding on giant sky clams? Nevadans would be wise to keep an eye on the skies.

– Grey Alien –

ROSWELL ROCK STAR

TYPE:	EARLIEST SIGHTING:
Alien-humanoid	1947
LOCATION:	**SIZE:**
Roswell, New Mexico	3–5 feet tall

You do not need to ask the people of Roswell, New Mex-
ico, if they believe in extraterrestrials. It's extremely evident
from the moment you enter the city that they truly, honestly,
sincerely believe in extraterrestrials'... power to bring in tourists. (That joke works better spoken than written.)

I think I got away with including the Hopkinsville Goblin
and the Flatwoods Monster and the Pascagoula Elephant Man
in this book, to help vary the monsters and because all of those
encounters have a cryptid-like mystery and panic surrounding them. But I understand if you want to refuse Roswell as a
cryptozoological site. You wouldn't even be wrong if you didn't
want to label what happened in Roswell a creature encounter at
all: it's a UFO sighting (and crash).

But here's the thing. Roswell has embraced the monsters
later speculations would put inside that crashed UFO—diminutive black-eyed, big-headed creatures knowns as "greys"—
better than any sasquatch city or lake monster land has ever
embraced their respective monsters. Extraterrestrial beings
are worked into the fabric of Roswell's identity and commerce

to the point that were you to pull that thread from the city, it would unravel into anonymity.

The transformation began in July 1947, when William Brazel, a rancher at the J. B. Forester Ranch about seventy-five miles north of Roswell, was inspecting the land after a violent storm the night before. He found one of the fields strewn with strange detritus—metallic foil, rubber, strange paper, sticks. He didn't really know at first what it could be. But then, at almost the exact same time, flying saucer mania hit the country.

Pilot Kenneth Arnold had, only weeks before, had a fateful encounter while flying near Mount Rainier in the state of Washington. He witnessed a formation of flying crescents shooting through the air in a way he described to the United Press as "like a saucer if you skip it across the water." That description mutated in the papers into the craft being shaped like flying saucers, and that misquote inspired the design of every extraterrestrial craft in every science fiction movie of the next decade: *The Day the Earth Stood Still, Plan 9 from Outer Space, Earth vs. the Flying Saucers, The Thing from Another World, Forbidden Planet.* Even beyond that decade, the *Millennium Falcon* and the starship *Enterprise* are both saucer-shaped spacecraft. Thousands of similar sightings worldwide were reported in the decades since and continue up to the present day, although in recent decades the term UFO has largely replaced *flying saucer* to include a variety of craft shapes.

With flying saucers firing the public consciousness, Brazel thought that the strange refuse he found might be the wreckage of one of them flying saucer things. He boxed it all up and took it to what was then called Roswell Army Air Field, or RAAF. Officials there, either keen to capitalize on the flying saucer craze or attempting to hide a secret project, sent out a press release stating that they had the remains of one of those saucers everybody was talking about. The local newspaper, the *Roswell Daily Record*, immediately ran with a story under the headline, RAAF CAPTURES FLYING SAUCER ON RANCH IN ROSWELL REGION.

It was a world-changer of a headline. But twenty-four hours later, this headline went out at the *Roswell Morning Dispatch*: ARMY DEBUNKS ROSWELL FLYING DISC AS WORLD SIMMERS WITH EXCITEMENT. The military explained that the wreckage was from not an alien craft but a weather balloon. A weather balloon! That whiplash of an about-face and the weakness of the explanation was so strange that it just seemed to everyone like something else going on. And something else *was* going on. The government was conducting a cover-up; it just wasn't necessarily covering up the existence of extraterrestrial life.

Project Mogul was an espionage initiative that lasted from 1947 to 1949. The military deployed high-altitude weather balloons equipped with sensors to detect sound waves that would carry in the upper atmosphere if Russia was performing experiments with nuclear bombs. And these weren't mere party balloons. Project Mogul balloons could be as long as 657 feet. In other words, they were spaceship-sized weather balloons. But that information wasn't declassified until half a century later in 1994.

Meanwhile, the original newspaper story seemed much more plausible than the idea that trained military personnel could mistake weather balloon parts for alien spacecraft parts. At the very least, it was much more interesting. Still, the story died down until 1978, when UFO researcher Stanton Friedman interviewed Major Jesse Marcel, who was part of the Air Force team that recovered the wreckage. Marcel claimed that the debris was indubitably extraterrestrial and that he had been ordered to keep it secret. That interview kindled an entire mythology that included government conspiracies, alien corpses pulled from the Roswell wreckage, and the super-secret Area 51 Air Force base in Nevada, where everything was hidden. Some even speculated that every major scientific advance for the next half century, from stealth aircraft to cell phones, was based on reverse-engineering the extraterrestrial technology that fell from the sky in July 1947.

And Roswell, New Mexico, rode that wave like they had alien technology implanted in their surfboards. They had to. A decade earlier the base had been decommissioned and the city was looking for ways to bolster its economy. They (crash) landed on alien-themed tourism.

The entire town belongs on Mars. It has a museum, of course—the Roswell UFO Museum and Research Center, which was founded by Glenn Dennis, a mortician who claimed to have knowledge of alien autopsies that the Air Force conducted in the aftermath of the crash. Roswell throws a UFO Festival every year. They sell enough alien souvenirs to clog a black hole. The seal of the city even features an alien. The city is so populated with statues of extraterrestrials that real extraterrestrials could hide in plain sight. The local McDonald's is shaped like a flying saucer. The Dunkin' Donuts/Baskin-Robbins sign is held up by a twenty-two-foot-tall alien. Interestingly, the city also has a statue of Robert Goddard, the father of rocketry, because he lived there in the 1930s and did some of his initial experiments in Roswell. Perhaps this explains why aliens would want to buzz by.

Whether extraterrestrial spacecraft or terrestrial spy balloon, something special happened to Roswell after that crash. It found its identity. And that identity is an alien monster.

The Cryptozoologist's Curse

For thousands of years, rumors of giant, dark-furred humanoids deep within the jungles of Africa were traded among soldiers and explorers, but the European scientific establishment treated those stories like it treated tales of sea monsters from sailors. That changed in 1859, when French explorer and zoologist Paul Du Chaillu returned to Europe from the west coast of Africa laden with skeletons, pelts, and sketches of the fabled gorilla.

A similar chain of events occurred with the Komodo dragon, a large, venomous lizard that lives on only a handful of small islands in Indonesia and wasn't known to the world at large until the early twentieth century. The same thing happened with the okapi, a hoofed quadruped from the Congo that looks like a combination of a giraffe, a zebra, and a deer. The giant squid was a myth until it was documented and promoted to specimen within marine biology. In Australia the idea of the platypus was so preposterous that European scientists declared it a fake even after handling a preserved body. I still have my doubts about it, honestly.

In every one of those stories (and others like them), a cryptid eventually becomes a regular animal. And that's kind of bad news for cryptozoologists. It's their curse. Because the discovery of a cryptid doesn't so much mean validation for the field as it does forfeiture. The moment an animal is proven to exist, the crypto part gets lopped off and the animal is neatly slotted into the field of zoology. That means, if we do ever find the Ozark Howler or a rougarou, they will get erased from the cryptid encyclopedias and added to the science textbooks.

Maybe that's why cryptozoology aficionados often focus their passions on the most improbable creatures. At least that way they get to keep them.

— Oregon Bigfoot —

BRONZE MEDALIST OF
THE BIGFOOT COAST

TYPE:
Humanoid

BIGFOOT FACT 1:
Oregon is the only state
with a permanent
bigfoot trap

BIGFOOT FACT 2:
The mascot for Oregon's
150th anniversary in 2009
was Seski the Sasquatch

Some say that bronze medal winners are the happiest on the podium. Gold winners are overwhelmed and under new pressures to continue to excel above all others. Silver is disappointed because it got so close to gold but didn't attain it. But bronze is just happy to be on the podium. And that's Oregon when it comes to the Bigfoot Coast: a happy and important part of it, even if they have to look up at the California and Washington flags above them.

According to the Bigfoot Field Researchers Organization—which ranks Washington and California as the first and second most bigfooted states in the union—the number of sightings in Oregon is relatively low, behind even the likes of Illinois, Florida, and Ohio. Maybe Oregonians just have a higher bar for what they legitimize as a sighting?

But Oregon is by no means bigfoot bereft. It has a museum, the North American Bigfoot Center in the town of Boring, where you can see life-sized replicas of the beast, watch a movie about it at its theater, and peruse various artifacts that include the ever-important bigfoot print casts. The Oregon Bigfoot Festival in Troutdale kicked off in 2017. The state also has statues scattered around its businesses and forests, although no real signature statue yet. It even has a bigfoot trap. Wait. What?

That's right: a bigfoot trap, located in the Rogue River-Siskiyou National Forest in Jacksonville, just north of the California border. There you'll find a wooden box the size of a large shed (about ten feet by ten feet) with a metal mesh door lifted to look inviting. Its thick planks are secured by metal bands and anchored to the ground with telephone poles. It certainly looks hefty enough to trap an eight-foot-tall, 350-pound primate.

And it's no press stunt. The trap was built in 1974 by the North American Wildlife Research Team (NAWRT), a small group dedicated to investigating bigfoot reports. A local miner named Perry Lovell reported seeing eighteen-inch footprints in the area. That report caught the attention Bob Patterson (of Patterson-Gimlin bigfoot footage fame) who convinced Ron Olson, founder of the NAWRT and a nature film producer, to look into it. And he looked into it and decided to create the world's first bigfoot trap.

The trap was a simple one. When a bigfoot tripped the door, it would drop and ring an alarm in a nearby cabin where a watchman was on guard. His job was to alert the NAWRT that their quarry had been caught. Members of the organization would then come to tranquilize, document, tag, and release the bigfoot. For six years, NAWRT kept that bigfoot trap in the forest stocked with animal carcasses. It was set off a few times, mostly by bears, although according to some reports it captured humans twice (a hippie one time and then a hunter another time). But it never caught a bigfoot.

The NAWRT no longer exists, and the watchman's cabin is a ruin these days, but the trap is still there (although the door is bolted open for safety). In 2005 a tree fell on it, but the trap was repaired the next year. These days, the trap is less remote than it used to be fifty years ago, and it takes a mere three-quarters of a mile walk to get there from the road. Meanwhile, the world's first and possibly only bigfoot trap just sits there, counting off the years until it gets old enough to become a National Historic Site or be boxed up and sent to the Smithsonian.

But it was a good try, Oregon. Because that's exactly how you beat Washington and California and nab the gold and all the bigfoot glory: you catch the thing.

–Living Dinosaurs–

CHRISTIAN CRYPTOZOOLOGY

TYPE:	**EARLIEST SIGHTING:**
Saurian	Prehistory
LOCATION:	**MATERIAL:**
Kachina Bridge and Black Dragon Canyon, Utah	Paintings and reliefs

Dinosaurs died out sixty-five million years ago from an asteroid to the face. And we miss them dearly. Not a single child hasn't fantasized about encountering a brontosaurus in their backyard or spotting a pterodactyl at the park. Then there are cryptozoologists, who are always saying, "What if?" when it comes to extinct creatures, even and sometimes especially dinosaurs (and I'm using the term broadly to also include large extinct marine and flying reptiles). And the only people more hopeful than children and cryptozoologists that dinosaurs are just playing hide and seek with science are young-earth creationist Christians, who posit that the Earth is merely between 6,000 and 10,000 years old, meaning dinosaurs and humans didn't miss each other on the evolution elevator.

While most lake and sea monsters would also fall into this category of "dinosaurs among us," stories of dry-land dinosaur cryptids are much rarer. Perhaps the best chance we have for a non-lake dinosaur who skipped class attendance is in Utah. Utah is full of dinosaurs. Or at least fossils of dinosaurs. It's home to Dinosaur National Monument, which includes over eight hundred important paleontological sites and thousands of dinosaur fossils. Although most of the Monument is in Colorado, its heart, the Dinosaur Quarry, is in Utah. And Utah has a couple of other places that make children, cryptozoologists, and young-earth Christians lean forward in their seats: Kachina Bridge and Black Dragon Canyon.

Kachina Bridge is one of three natural stone bridges at Natural Bridges National Monument in San Juan County. That 204-foot-long span of sandstone is the second-largest of the three and arcs 210 feet above the ground. The surface under that bridge, on the flanks of the supporting rock, is decorated by a panoply of pictographs and petroglyphs (paintings and carvings, respectively) of dancing people, symbols, and animals like bighorn sheep created by Ancestral Puebloans over the centuries. Among the depictions are, according to certain creationists and cryptozoologists, four potential dinosaur images, only one of which is passionately argued to be such—a long-necked sauropod like an apatosaurus or diplodocus.

The image is about ten feet off the ground and in weak contrast against the red rock. Still, the petroglyph looks remarkably like a dinosaur straight out of a child's coloring book, with a humped back, a long neck topped by a small head, and a long tail that lifts at the end like the terrible lizard is trying to wag it. There's no context for the shape—it's not surrounded by hunters with spears and it's not in a herd of other sauropods or fighting off a T-rex. It's just there.

Answers in Genesis, a nonprofit organization dedicated to the intellectual defense of the Christian faith, regularly upholds the Kachina Bridge image as a dinosaur. The organization believes that the artists were drawing from their own experience and that, in the words of a 2020 Answers in Genesis article by Troy Lacey and Bodie Hodge, "the [Ancestral Puebloan] people clearly saw living sauropods." That's sixty-five million years after scientists say the dinosaurs were all boiled off.

In 2011, Phil Senter, a professor at Fayetteville State University in North Carolina, and Sally Cole, an archeological consultant, published a paper in the peer-reviewed journal *Palaeontologia Electronica* debunking the four dinosaurs as mud stains and misinterpreted images. They spent particular effort on the "creationist poster child" that is the sauropod image. The researchers examined the image with binoculars and telephoto lenses under different lighting conditions and determined that the sauropod is actually three abstract images (a sinuous line, a U-shaped line, and a spiral) and a mud stain that have been altered by age and weather and are subject to the phenomenon of pareidolia—the human penchant for seeing images or patterns everywhere. A writer at Answers in Genesis named Ishmael Abrahams quickly rebutted the paper, concluding: "In light of the poor quality of the research and arguments, Senter and Cole have brought nothing of substance to refute the idea that this Native American petroglyph . . . is best explained as a dinosaur."

Similarly contentious rock art can be found 170 miles north of Kachina Bridge in Black Dragon Canyon, near the town of Green River. A short hike through the canyon brings visitors to a rock face decorated with a wide range of Native American pictographs and petroglyphs, including one that looks like a giant flying creature, wings spread, that gave the canyon its name and gave creationists the opportunity to claim it as firsthand evidence that pterosaurs overlapped with humans. Back at Answers in Genesis, a 2002 article by a man named Bill Johnson stated that, based on this image, Native Americans "apparently saw a bird-like creature with enormous wings, a tail, a long neck and beak, and a vertical head crest, which some flying reptiles sported."

In 2015, researchers Jean-Loïc Le Quellec, Paul Bahn, and Marvin Rowe published an article in the peer-reviewed journal *Antiquity* called "The Death of a Pterodactyl." In it, the authors used X-ray fluorescence to bring out the iron in the red pigments of the paintings to distinguish paint from weathering, revealing what they believe is not a flying reptile, but a typical canyon scene of human figures and non-dinosaur animals that have eroded and blended together over time. They concluded, "By removing interpretational bias, the new technology finally lays to rest the Black Dragon Canyon pterosaur." Lacey and Hodge at Answers in Genesis responded to this study as well: "The 'new' images that are formed by their analysis through computer technology similar to Photoshop are completely ridiculous looking. . . . Those arguing against the pterosaur interpretation have a vested interest in 'disproving' pterosaurs coexisted with mankind."

If the scientists are correct, it means a lot of disappointed people: those looking for fuel to fire their young imaginations, those questing for evidence of overlooked species, and especially those looking for proof of an infant planet. But the biggest loser is the state of Utah itself, because "Dinosaurs Live Here" would be a great motto to punch onto its license plates.

–Jackalope–

THE CUTEST CRYPTID

TYPE:	**EARLIEST SIGHTING:**
Mammalian	1934
LOCATION:	**NOTABLE FEATURES:**
Douglas, Wyoming	Rabbit-like body; branching antlers

You'd think there would be no way to improve on the jackrabbit: elegant ears, twitching nose, soft fur, fluffy tail, darling jumps. There's a reason why it's a beloved pet and a major holiday mascot and an iconic Warner Bros. cartoon character. But then the jackalope came along, and we were all like, "Oh yeah. Antlers. Even better."

The name jackalope is a portmanteau of jackrabbit and antelope, although the physical form of the creature isn't so evenly divided. The jackalope is simply a jackrabbit with branching antlers on its head in proportion to its small size. Illustrations of horned hares in scientific texts go back centuries, but the first sighting in North America was supposedly by John Colter: explorer, member of the Lewis and Clark Expedition, and the first white man to set foot in what would one day be the state of Wyoming, home of the jackalope.

But giving jackrabbits head-racks may not be simply an inevitable outcome of human imagination. Many believe that (and we're about to get sad here for the rest of the paragraph) early myths of horned hares came from actual sightings of ordinary hares in the wild who were afflicted with Shope papilloma virus, a condition in which horn-like carcinomas grow out of an animal's head and face. If the carcinomas grow large enough, they can interfere with the hare's ability to eat, causing starvation. Don't Google those images.

However, it wasn't until the early twentieth century that the creature was named and adorable versions started appearing in bars and hotels and shops—in taxidermy form. In 1934, taxidermy aficionados and brothers Ralph and Douglas Herrick returned to their Douglas, Wyoming, home after an exhausting day of hunting. They were in a rush to get some food that didn't have to be gutted and skinned, so they dropped off the day's quarry with little thought and rushed to the dinner table. When they returned, they noticed a rabbit carcass had fallen next to a set of deer antlers. It was a "you got chocolate in my peanut butter" moment and they were inspired to start making what would come to be called jackalopes: mounted hares with deer antlers attached. The first specially sewn specimen went to hotelier Roy Ball, who paid a rumored ten bucks for it and put it up in his Hotel LaBonte downtown, jump-starting the myth that Ball was the first person to catch one of these creatures.

Soon, the jackalope became a national phenomenon. You only had to see one of these darling dead animals to want one. Taxidermied jackalopes appeared as whimsical decorations in restaurants and bars and hotels and gift shops. In the decades since, the jackalope has lent its image to sports mascots, TV characters, product brands, and toys. Tall tales sprang up about its habits and abilities—that it only breeds during lightning flashes, that it likes whiskey and can mimic human voices, and that it uses those antlers to gore predators when threatened.

According to an article in the *Casper Star Tribune*, jackalope hunters should wear stovepipes on their legs as protection.

But home is where the hare is, and Douglas, Wyoming, is the jackalope's home. You can find jackalopes there in ways that you cannot find them anywhere else in the country. For instance, in Jackalope Square is an eight-foot-tall statue of the cryptid that was once the tallest jackalope statue in the country. It held the record until Douglas one-upped itself by erecting a fifteen-foot-tall statue at the Douglas Railroad Interpretive Center. Every year in June, the town hosts Jackalope Days, with live music and food and vendors enough to rival the state fair. The highway proudly bears signs warning of jackalope crossing. Heck, the town slogan of Douglas is HOME OF THE JACKALOPE. WE KNOW JACK. Every year the Douglas Chamber of Commerce offers hunting licenses for jackalopes (only good for June 31, and trappers are forbidden to use booze to bait the beasts).

And the rest of the state is catching on. The Wyoming state lottery uses the jackalope as its mascot and logo, and Dubois, Wyoming, boasts the world's largest jackalope exhibit at the Jackalope Travel Stop. The gas station/country store/museum features two horse-sized jackalopes you can ride for photo ops (one fiberglass and one furry), a jackalope-shaped disco ball, and plenty of souvenirs to purchase.

It seems like such a small thing, a jackrabbit with antlers, but who can predict what will capture the fancy of fickle humans? So the next time you see a furry face with a button nose and horns mounted above a bar, raise a glass to weird beasts and the strange stories they represent.

Epilogue: Keep Searching!

We have come to the end of our parade of cryptids. I hope you enjoyed every monstrous float. And I hope that you find some value in the idea that cryptids have significance beyond whether or not they physically exist: that they are symbols of hope that our planet is capable of unlimited surprises; that they can rally a spiraling town by bestowing both an identity and an economy; that they help preserve stories from history that would otherwise be lost. Seen this way, cryptids are more important culturally than scientifically. But the best thing about cryptids, for me, is that they're just a lot of fun.

My daughters accompanied me on many of my journeys to see these cryptid tourist spots. Telling them about a new monster on any given day felt like introducing them to a new Santa Claus. Other parents, when they found out what I was working on, asked me to recommend places to take their cryptid-obsessed kids. Cryptids offer so many opportunities for human enjoyment, inspiration, and connection. I read about scientists going into their chosen fields after developing a passion for nature and animals from learning about cryptids as children. I've seen cryptid fans who bond, not over finding cryptids, but just over the idea of them. They're excuses to hang out online and at conventions and on road trips with like-minded weirdos. Why talk about politics when you can talk about that time a lizard man attacked a car to get at the bag of Filet-O-Fish sandwiches inside? These monsters are the in-jokes of these groups, the shibboleths, the secret handshakes. If you can have fun with the idea of a hodag, you can be a friend of mine.

But despite all these benefits, cryptids are endangered. The longer we go without a bigfoot corpse, the harder it is to insist it exists. The further in time we travel away from the Beast of Busco, the easier it is to forget that the sightings ever happened. The towns that celebrate their monsters keep them alive as symbols when they expire as possibilities. And we all need monsters. How impoverished is Greek culture without minotaurs or centaurs? Or Chinese culture without dragons? Native Americans without wendigo and skinwalkers? Where is Catholicism without its devils and angels? Sailors without their sea serpents and kraken? Children without boogeymen in their closets? Sure, we have fictional monsters in our movies and books, but a thousand Frankensteins and King Kongs and Grendels weigh far less than a single monster that is "based on a true story."

And the stories are true. People saw things. They panicked. They feared for their lives and their notions of reality. In each of these stories, *something* happened. Maybe it was just owls instead of goblins in Kentucky, but that strange battle still went down. Maybe the Mothman was just a sandhill crane, but books weren't written and movies made and museums opened because a town was terrified by a big bird. It was terrified by a bigger idea than that (also, possibly, by a six-foot-tall humanoid insect).

I asked Loren Coleman (I promise this is the last time I mention him in this book) what happens if we don't find a bigfoot's corpse. After all, Coleman has been in the field for sixty years, and in that time there hasn't been a ton of progress in finding the classic cryptids. In fact, evidence has only mounted against them. The question didn't faze him; it was no threat to a life dedicated to cryptozoology.

"A lot of discoveries have been made," he told me. "And people forget about that because they move on—okapis, coelacanth, gorilla, beaked whales, giant squid." All of these creatures were once believed to be mythical, until they were discovered by scientists. "A prime example is *Homo floresiensis*. The Hobbit," he continued. He explained that the stories of little people—whether they're Menehune or puckwudgies or leprechauns—had a basis in truth. "Now we have proof that these little people were real, but they're not part of cryptozoology anymore. They're part of anthropology. As to bigfoot, maybe we have already found it. There are all these fossils we have in museum storage rooms. Who knows what we'll discover? A few months ago all the media outlets were talking about the giant skull found in a well in China. Some of my friends immediately sent me a note, 'Could this be a bigfoot skull?'"

In the end, the charge of cryptozoology is not, "I swear I saw something," as it is often portrayed, but "keep searching!" Even if you don't find Bigfoot, you'll find something worthwhile. Guaranteed.

Selected Sites & Festivals

Silver Lake Serpent

Country Club Statue: 3820 Club Rd., Perry, NY

Splash Pad Serpent: 121 Lake St., Perry, NY

Downtown statue: Main St. and Lake St., Perry, NY

Whitehall Bigfoot

Downtown Statue: Skenesborough Dr., Whitehall, NY

Bigfoot Wine and Liquor Statue: 132 Broadway St., Whitehall, NY

Vermont Marble Granite, Slate & Soapstone Co. Statue and Giftshop: 10014 US-4, Whitehall, NY

Skene Valley Country Club Statue: 129 County Route 9A, Whitehall, NY

Sasquatch Festival and Calling Contest: September (Whitehall, NY)

Champ

Monument: Perkins Pier, Burlington, VT

ECHO, Leahy Center for Lake Champlain: 1 College St., Burlington, VT

Welcome Sign and Sightings Board: Main St., Port Henry, NY

Champ Day: Summer (Port Henry, NY)

Historic Marker: Cumberland Head Rd., Plattsburg, NY

Wampahoofus

Wampahoofus Trail: Mount Mansfield, Stowe, VT

Jersey Devil

Lucille's Country Cooking and Statue: 1496 Main St., Barnegat, NJ

International Cryptozoology Museum

International Cryptozoology Museum: 32 Resurgam Pl., Portland, ME

International Cryptozoology Museum Bookstore: 585 Hammond St., Bangor, ME

Snarly Yow

Historic Placard: 6132 Old National Pike, Boonsboro, MD

Snallygaster

Mural Series: Main St., Sykesville, MD

Gloucester Sea Serpent

Mural: Cressy Beach, Hough Ave., Gloucester, MA

Statue: 27 Pleasant St., Gloucester, MA

Albatwitch

Chickies Rock: 880 Chickies Hill Rd., Columbia, PA

Albatwitch Day: October (Columbia, PA)

Fouke Monster

Fouke Monster Mart: 104 US-71, Fouke, AR

Fouke Monster Festival: Summer (Fouke, AR)

Wampus Cat

Statue: 2300 Prince St., Conway, AR

Mothman

Statue: Main St. and 4th St., Point Pleasant, WV

Mothman Museum: 400 Main St., Point Pleasant, WV

TNT Bunkers: Potters Creek Rd., Point Pleasant, WV

Silver Bridge Memorial: Main St. and 6th St., Point Pleasant, WV

Mothman Festival: Third weekend in September (Point Pleasant, WV)

Flatwoods Monster

Flatwoods Monster Museum: 208 Main St., Sutton, WV

Welcome Sign: Dyer Hill Rd. and Sutton Ln., Sutton, WV

The Spot Dairy Bar: 922 Gauley Tpke., Flatwoods, WV

Flatwoods Monster Fest: September (Flatwoods, WV)

Skunk Ape

Skunk Ape Research Headquarters: 40904 Tamiami Trail E., Ochopee, FL

Lizard Man

Harry and Harry Too: 719 Sumter Hwy., Bishopville, SC

South Carolina Cotton Museum: 121 W Cedar Ln., Bishopville, SC

Scape Ore Swamp Bridge: Browntown Rd., Bishopville, SC

Festival: Summer (Bishopville, SC)

Altamaha-ha

Darien-McIntosh Regional Visitor Information Center (Statue): 1111 Magnolia Bluff Way, SW, Darien, GA

Moon-Eyed People

Cherokee County Historical Museum Statue: 87 Peachtree St., Murphy, NC

Fort Mountain State Park Ruins: 181 Fort Mountain Park Rd., Chatsworth, GA

Beast of Bladenboro

Beast Fest: Fall (Bladenboro, NC)

Woodbooger

Woodbooger Grill: 921 Park Ave. NW, Norton, VA

Bigfoot Statue and Sanctuary: Flag Rock Recreation Area, Norton, VA

Woodbooger Festival: October (Norton, VA)

Rougarou

Marie Laveau's House of Voodoo: 628 Bourbon St., New Orleans, LA
Audubon Zoo Exhibit: 6500 Magazine St., New Orleans, LA
Historic Placard: 114 Tourist Dr., Gray, LA
Statue: Park Ave. and Suthon Ave., Houma, LA
Rougarou Fest: October (Houma, LA)

Chupacabra

San Antonio Zoo Exhibit: 3903 N. St. Mary's St., San Antonio, TX
Kingdom Zoo Wildlife Center Exhibit: 2300 41st St., Orange, TX

Minnesota Iceman

Museum of the Weird: 412 E. 6th St., Austin, TX

Pascagoula Elephant Man

Historic Placard: 3776 Frederic St., Pascagoula, MS

Hopkinsville Goblin

Little Green Men Days Festival: August (Kelly, KY)
UFO Installation: 7440 Old Madisonville Rd., Hopkinsville, KY

Piasa Bird

Cliff Painting: Highway 100, one mile north of Alton, IL
Southwestern High School Sculpture: 8226 Rt. 111, Piasa, IL

Beast of Busco

Churubusco Community Park Statue: John Krieger Dr., Churubusco, IN
Downtown Statue: E. State Rd. and U.S. 33 N., Churubusco, IN
Fulk Lake: Madden Rd. and N. County Line Road W., Churubusco, IN
Turtle Days Festival: June (Churubusco, IN)

Van Meter Visitor

Van Meter Visitor Festival: September (Van Meter, IA)

Pope Lick Monster

Pope Lick Trestle: 3098 S. Pope Lick Rd., Louisville, KY

Nain Rouge

Marche du Nain Rouge: March (Cass Corridor, Detroit, MI)

Thunderbird

Thunderbird Sculpture: 2190 River Rd., Bismarck, ND

Writing Rock State Historic Site: 94th St. NW and 145 Ave. NW, Grenora, ND

Dahl Bigfoot

Statue: 121 Roy Street Highway 16A, Keystone, SD

Peninsula Python

Peninsula Library and Historical Society: 6105 Riverview Rd., Peninsula, OH

Peninsula Python Day: July (Peninsula, OH)

Underwater Panther

Effigy Mound: 417 Bryn Du Dr., Granville, OH

Dawson Gnome

Statues: Yellowstone Trail and 1st St., Dawson, MN

Dawson Public Library: 676 Pine St., Dawson, MN

Riverfest: June (Dawson, MN)

Beast of Bray Road

Statue: W3324 Bray Rd., Elkhorn, WI

Hodag

Chamber of Commerce Statue: 450 W. Kemp St., Rhinelander, WI

Rhinelander Logging Museum: Martin Lynch Dr., Rhinelander, WI

The Hodag Store: 538 Lincoln St., Rhinelander, WI

Rhinelander High School: 665 Coolidge Ave., Rhinelander, WI

Hodag Heritage Days: May (Rhinelander, WI)

Rhinelapus

The monster itself: 1668 US-8, Monico, WI

Mount Horeb Troll

Trollway: Main St., Mount Horeb, WI

Scandinavian Winter Festival: February (Mount Horeb, WI)

California Bigfoot

Bigfoot Steakhouse: 19 Willow Way, Willow Creek, CA

Willow Creek China Flat Museum: 38949 CA-299, Willow Creek, CA

Mural: 39168 CA-299, Willow Creek, CA

Bigfoot Discovery Museum: 5497 Hwy. 9, Felton, CA

Bigfoot Daze: September (Willow Creek, CA)

Menehune

Poliahu Heiau: 5568 Kuamoo Rd., Kapaʻa, HI

Kīkīaola Ditch: Menehune Rd., Waimea, HI

Ulupō Heiau: 1200 Kailua Rd., Kailua, HI

Menehune Fishpond: 2458 Hulemalu Rd., Lihue, HI

Washington Bigfoot

Harry and the Hendersons Filming Site and Statue: 50000 Stevens Pass Hwy., Gold Bar, WA

Cement Statue: 9745 Spirit Lake Hwy., Toutle, WA

Sharlie

Playground Statue: 335 W Lake St., McCall, ID

McCall Winter Carnival: January/February (McCall, ID)

Shunka Warak'in

Madison Valley History Association Museum: 447 State
Highway 287 South, Ennis, MT

Grey Alien

Flying Saucer McDonald's: 720 N. Main St., Roswell, NM

Alien Dunkin Donuts: 800 N. Main St., Roswell, NM

International UFO Museum and Research Center: 114 N.
Main St., Roswell, NM

UFO Festival: July (Roswell, NM)

Oregon Bigfoot

North American Bigfoot Center: 31297 SE, US-26, Boring, OR

Bigfoot Trap: Upper Applegate Rd., Applegate, OR

Jackalope

World's Largest Jackalope Statue: 121 Brownfield Rd.,
Douglas, WY

Jackalope Square and Statue: 3rd St. and Center St., Douglas, WY

Jackalope Exhibit: 404 W. Rams Horn St., Dubois, WY

Jackalope Days: June (Douglas, WY)

Further Reading

For a complete list of references consulted, visit
quirkbooks.com/unitedstatesofcryptids.

Blackburn, L. *Lizard Man: The True Story of the Bishopville Monster.* San Antonio, TX: Anomalist Books, 2013.

Coleman, L. *Mysterious America.* New York: Pocket Books, 2001.

Coleman, L., and J. Clark. *Cryptozoology A to Z: The Encyclopedia of Loch Monsters, Sasquatch, Chupacabras, and Other Authentic Mysteries of Nature.* New York: Touchstone, 2014.

Cox, W. T. *Fearsome Creatures of the Lumberwoods: With a Few Desert and Mountain Beasts.* Sacramento, CA: Bishop Pub. Co., 1984. Originally published 1910.

Dickey, C. *The Unidentified: Mythical Monsters, Alien Encounters, and Our Obsession with the Unexplained.* New York: Penguin Books, 2021.

Eberhart, G. M. *Mysterious Creatures: A Guide to Cryptozoology.* Santa Barbara, CA: ABC-CLIO, 2013.

Godfrey, L. S. *American Monsters: A History of Monster Lore, Legends, and Sightings in America.* New York: Penguin Books, 2014.

Godfrey, L. S. *The Beast of Bray Road: Tailing Wisconsin's Werewolf.* Self-published, 2015.

Gosselin, B., and S. Gosselin. *Abair Road: The True Story.* Self-published, 2018.

Keel, J. A. *The Mothman Prophecies.* New York: Tor, 2013.

Lewis, C., and K. L. Nelson. *Wendigo Lore: Monsters, Myths, and Madness*. Eau Claire, WI: On the Road Publications, 2020.

Lewis, C., N. Voss, and K. L. Nelson. *The Van Meter Visitor: A True and Mysterious Encounter with the Unknown*. Eau Claire, WI: On the Road Publications, 2013.

Loxton, D., and D. R. Prothero. *Abominable Science!: Origins of the Yeti, Nessie, and Other Famous Cryptids*. New York: Columbia University Press, 2015.

Nickell, J. *Real-Life X-Files: Investigating the Paranormal*. Lexington: University Press of Kentucky, 2001.

Tryon, H. H. *Fearsome Critters*. Cornwall, NY: The Idlewild Press, 1939.

Acknowledgments

I t would have been impossible to corral the more than seventy monsters captured within these pages without the following sources of support: my editor, Rebecca Gyllenhaal, who—Tom Slick–like—sent me on this expedition; my agent, Alex Slater, to whom this book is dedicated; my wife, Lindsey, and daughters Esme, Hazel, and Olive, not only for their unceasing encouragement of my writing life but for enthusiastically accompanying me on my many visits to Cryptid Towns. I should have bought them double the souvenirs.

I'd like to thank Adam Perry, who took me to Chickies Rock in Pennsylvania to hunt for albatwitches; Chad Abramovich for leading me across the icy and treacherous realm of the wampahoofus in Vermont; and Dave Goudsward, for being gracious and receptive to all my ridiculous late-night DMs about cryptids ("Hey, ever heard of a woodbooger?"). I'd also like to thank Loren Coleman and Sarah Cooper for being a part of this book and sharing with me their passion for cryptids.

I owe so much to the team at Quirk who made my words into both better words and a piece of art—Kassie Andreadis and Jane Morley had to, among other difficult tasks, almost invent a new set of grammar rules for so many strange monster names. And thanks to Elissa Flanigan for the gorgeous cover design, John McGurk for production management, and Derek Quinlan for his spectacular artwork that is one hundred percent the reason you gave this compendium a chance.

Finally, this book would not exist without all those who, over the centuries, had the courage to share their monster encounters, no matter how bizarre.